Jumpstart to Software Quality Assurance

Vishnuvarthanan Moorthy

ISBN: **149120351X**
ISBN-13: **978-1491203514**

DEDICATION TO

The Supreme Power!

He Creates, He Maintains, He Destroys and He Authors!

CONTENTS

PREFACE

Software Industry has grown a lot in the last few decades, and there are many players are there in the market. Most of the software is made in an unknown country and by unknown people. Though cost and people competency are the major influencing factor for determining, who will produce the software or provide the service, in reality almost all the contracts are made by looking at delivery methodologies, process maturity and demonstration of technical capabilities. Most of the contracts are not awarded for people skill, considering no one knows which person is working in the service provider organization. The contracts are awarded based on Processes, past performance and technical understanding, which the service providers demonstrate along with good costing. It's because the only way a client can believe the unknown you is, by knowing your way of working and your processes. You would agree, most of your clients are not your neighbor, friend or relative, so that they can blindly give the work order to you! Neither all our companies are doing Research projects, so that based on people competency we are awarded projects!

Who develops these processes, who maintains them and how come these processes have become matured, and how you are able to demonstrate your processes and delivery methodologies are in par or better than your competitors, who are those people, who makes your prestigious client to believe you… There are many, like Operational teams, center of excellences, heroic sales team and vital management team, and beyond this, we all would agree it's the Software Quality Assurance team which plays key role in ensuring process implementation, stability and capability. This book is written for those who are aspiring to take up a role in Software Quality Assurance or those who wants to set up a function and get the benefit out of it or for those who wants to understand, how practically the Software Quality Assurance function works. Today, Software Quality Analyst (SQA) role is a key component in any successful service provider's delivery system.

To perform as SQA, it's expected the person develops all around competency required for that role in the initial years. As they get experienced they can concentrate on specialized areas to improve their competency and contribute to the organizations. Many a times, we see the new SQA's struggle to get a complete a view of their roles and knowledge areas in Software Quality Assurance. Lack of complete understanding on software quality assurance affects their productivity and career path. This book is intended to provide those details, which are essential for Jumpstart to Software Quality Assurance. A SQA can gain experience by working with projects, but may not learn the basics, responsibilities and techniques/methods required to perform in his/her role! This book provides you the theoretical and pragmatic view on Software Quality Assurance!

1 QUALITY FUNDAMENTALS

We will ask the difficult question to ourselves, what is Quality? Why this question is difficult, because there are so many variant in its definition. Also quality is most subjectively used word in this word. We all use this word commonly in our life and I am sure frequency is also high. However in a given condition if we show a product to multiple people their evaluation of quality on the product will differ much. For example if we show a low end smart mobile phone costing around 150$ to ten people, their understanding on quality will vary, and some will concentrating on camera features, some will be on Audio quality, some on video quality, some on feather touch quality and so on. Quality in this case is based on different features offered for the price range, and comparison with similar products available in market, and what user thinks as friendly interface to them. For someone who is looking for high end features in camera in that phone, it's not of quality and for someone who is expecting high end audio this mobile is not of quality. What this tells us is, Quality is subjective in nature and also it's determined by comparing similar product/service available in that range of cost. However the International bodies and Quality Gurus have worked greatly in this area to reduce subjectivity and bring in the perspective with which every product/service can define Quality in that particular instance. They have defined few of the characteristics we should consider, while fixing boundaries and target for our product/service Quality.

ISO definition for quality is, "The totality of features and characteristics of a product or service that bears on its ability to satisfy the stated and implied

Needs" which tells us, as long as the product is meeting the agreed and implicit requirements, we can assume it's of quality. Similarly the degree to which the product's characteristics excel also determines quality as not all the characteristics are having equal importance. Some of them might be must have and some might be like to have, and we would definitely want the must have features satisfied by the product or service. We all know most of the basic software like word, excel, etc are having so many features in them, but we would concentrate on few features like word style, formatting, and review options more and we may use very rarely the export to blog, PDF, etc. When we have word document creator software which doesn't have many options in formatting, we would not prefer, even it has direct export to social media sites. What it means is, identify the right features and satisfying them is also part of Quality.

Quality Gurus:
Phil Crosby

- 'Conformance with requirements'

If your product meets the stated and implied requirements, it means your product is of Quality. When we buy a television we see the features listed, if our requirements and the features are in line we go for that television, else we choose some other one which is very close to our expectations. However if we don't what's written in the feature list, than the product has not met the requirements, and we claim it's not of quality.

Juran

- Definition: "fitness for purpose"

- Quality does not happen by accident

- Quality is a result of intention and actions

This is the most used definition in our normal life. We don't care what's written in the product or service description, but what we care is, whether this is of real use. Assume we bought a PDF software and most of the time we use PDF conversion to ensure the document is not editable and also we expect when we convert them from basic format (.doc, .xls, etc) to PDF it becomes smaller in size, so that we can mail it. Assume the product is converting the documents well as PDF but gives you something bulky in size and you don't have option to reduce the size of final output, then it's of very less use, in fact we will search for something which is fitting our purpose.

Other than Art, I don't think in engineering we can say quality happens by accident. Even in art, now a day there is some level of planning and technical perfection has been brought intentionally.

Ishikawa

- Quality is beyond the quality of product. Quality of after sales service, quality of management, quality of the company and quality of people - all matter

It's simple, when we buy a car, we just don't say the product is awesome, we wait for the servicing, we wait for replacements and then we say this is a good product. Assume you got the Costliest car in this world, but the side mirror which got damaged by a motorist is not available for replacement and you need to wait for another few months or the service person has to travel from some other country to replace it. How do you feel about your product? Most of us will feel it's a pain. Assume you have bought a top selling Antivirus product, and its license key is not working or registering and you are trying to contact their support team, there is no email/communication from them for 2 weeks, what will you do with this product. In fact we assume the product sells well, because it has good service also.

The Other important person in this Quality world is Dr. Edward Deming and his definitions and experimentations are world famous and have changed the Quality Industry a lot. His 14 principles of quality is a separate book and we would recommend the readers to spent time on those writings. The fact is most of the organizations still having basic problems with quality and many of them have been already pointed out by Deming.

There is something which Deming has given to the world, which will make him always the greatest is the PDCA cycle.

P - Plan

D- Do

C- Check

A-Act

This is a wheel, Plan->Do->Check->Act->Plan

For improving any system or feature or activity or anything, this cycle of activities are basic.

In our normal life we keep applying this principle without our knowledge on daily basis. If we go to buy groceries in a shop, we normally plan what to buy and take stock at our home, and we add products to our cart, and we check whether we bought all the required products and if not we go take the relevant products and add it to our cart. This is the same for going to a bank or purchasing a camera or anything. When we don't follow this cycle, we have more chance of not meeting our own expectations or failing in something.

This is the wheel which is adopted in many process improvement models and standards like ISO as basis. Though there are many concepts evolved with variations with this base model, this one remains the basis and most used improvement wheel.

Based on all these views, we can define quality something like this,

Quality is the degree to which product or service possesses a desired combination of attributes –

— *C: Capability (F: Functionality)*

— *U: Usability*

— *S: Scalability*

— *P: Performance (E: Efficiency)*

— *R: Reliability*

— *I: Install-ability (P: Portability)*

— *S: Security*

— *M: Maintainability*

And there are always two views exists with Quality,

— *Producer's view:*   *Meeting Requirements*

— *Customer's view:*   *Fit for use*

In the previous examples also we saw, that producers collect requirements from known client or from potential clients through market research and try to meet those requirements. However for a customer it's always, how good the product meets their requirements. In the of example of mobile phone, where every producer try to determine the requirements well and almost of all of them might be meeting what they identified as requirements, but customer feels only few products are really fit for them to use, and that's the reason few are sold well and few are not. The one, who tries to reduce this gap, eventually makes success with their product or service.

Quality Assurance and Quality Control:

There is always some level of confusion in using these terminologies in Industry and it's not the confusion with the activities, but it's more to do with the perspective with which they look at the Quality Activities. First of all, to achieve quality it's important to have the right intentions, plan and execution to prevent non conformities, and meet requirements and achieve planned services. The activities to achieve quality can be primarily split in to Quality Assurance and Quality Control.

Quality Assurance is defined as set of activities whose purpose is to demonstrate that an entity will meet all requirements. Quality control is defined as set of activities whose purpose is to ensure that all requirements are met in the final product/service.

Quality Assurance	*Quality Control*

Preventive in nature	Detection in nature
From beginning of a project and in beginning of a phase	In the later part of project and in mostly end phase activity
Process based	Product based
Process Quality Assurance team is involved	Product/Service Quality validation team is involved (Ex: Testers, Reviewers)
Organizational wide Strategy	Product/Service wise strategy

Quality Assurance is the activity which a Software Quality Analyst is expected to perform. Some organizations call the testing activities as software quality assurance and the testers as Software Quality Analyst, however this is not an industry wide practice and most of the standards or models don't recommend testers to be called as Software Quality Analyst or Quality Analyst.

As we saw in the table the Quality assurance activities are at organizational level and process based it's important for us to understand, how they are built at organizational level and what components are part of it. Be clear, organizational wide Quality Assurance strategy is built, however it's also tailored and applied at project level also. The organizational wide strategies help to ensure consistency across different products/projects in the organization.

Wherever we use the term Product in this book, please consider Services also along with it.

Quality Management System and its components:

This is the famous word in the Quality Assurance world, "Quality Management System (QMS)". What is a QMS? It's nothing but the existing management system in your organization, which has processes, people and tools which are aligned to achieve Quality in the delivery and where required additional capabilities (like roles/tools) are added to ensure that your system is aligned and working towards achieving quality. When we say financial management system, legal management system and so on, in an organization, it doesn't mean a new management team, or documents or tools, it's the Organizational management system component which is aligned to take care of a particular aspect like finance or legal needs.

Also be clear that many people think QMS is nothing but set of documents, which is not the reality. A QMS contains Processes, Tools, Roles and Responsibility, Policy, objectives and so on. Any component in the organization which is contributing to the achievement of Quality in the product/service is part of Quality Management System.

Since we use the word "System" many times here, what is a system? It's a set of interrelated components which along with relevant resources, process the inputs as expected output. In our body we have digestion system, respiratory system and blood circulation system, etc. They are system as they perform certain processes with their interrelated components using relevant resources and achieve the expected output.

Now we have used the word "process" few times here, what is a process? Its set of sequential activities performed to achieve desired results using the relevant resources. A system normally consists of multiple processes. In the case of Respiratory system in our body, the body inhales air is a process, the body separates the compounds in air is a process, the compounds are mixed and segregated from blood is a process and body exhales air is another process. If we want to split inhaling process in to smaller process, we can do, that's a sub process. In this case, nose inhales air, air is filtered in nostrils, air passes through the respiratory tube, air enters inside lung all can be sub processes. So who decides what sub process is and what is process? To tell you simply, we do write only processes and we use processes in normal life, however when we want to understand deeper the activities and control it we split the smaller activities as sub processes. You can even call the entire respiratory system as one process in body. Ultimately it's the criticality which decides what the level of process is.

With this understanding let's see the components in Quality Management System, which are usually part of it,

There are many Levels of documents are part of Quality Management System. Ideally these documents are created from Level 1 and reaches up to Level 4. This is simple, whatever your organization is doing and intent to do or the way you want to work, all these are documented (it can be electronic copy/hard copy/audio/video/automated tool or any other useful methods) and made available for your employees, so that all of them follow similar working method. In this case Level 1 is Quality Manual, which is the Apex document in the Quality Management System. Level 2 is methods and processes which are used by the employees to deliver outputs in their area. Level 3 is Guidelines, checklists and templates, they are used most often on daily basis and all of them help to ensure consistency in the information the deliverable contains. Level 4 is Records and Documents for validation, they help us as evidence of activity which is useful for any reference and proof.

Quality Manual:

Every Quality management system contains quality manual as apex document, which provides detail on how the quality policy, objectives are achieved in the organization. The scope of processes, process architecture, and detail of every process is detailed in the manual. The Quality manual helps anyone to understand how the system is defined and helps to navigate the processes.

Quality Manual contains the following sections,

1.0 Introduction

1.1 Purpose

1.2 Scope

1.3 References

7.6 Guidelines

7.7 Standards

Annexure: Process Architecture

Annexure: Process Details

Quality Policy:

This is the intention and direction of an Organization, in regard to achieve quality, as formally expressed by the top management.

Example: "Effective processes and competent people usage to deliver successful products with high Quality to our clients"- this can be a policy of an organization, which expresses how they want to achieve the quality and the means (Effective Process and competent people)

Process:

Set of activities performed in pre identified manner to convert inputs to required outputs, with usage of relevant resources.

Process will vary based on the activities sequence change or alteration of resources or input variation, etc. For an example, if we take cheese making process, the material/ingredients used is same and overall set of activities are also same, but just with variation in usage of material, application of resources (like heat/days storage/etc), there are more than 200 types cheese produced. What it means is the process in fact varies and 200 types of processing happen. What it tells is, a Process is with fixed steps, method and resources, so that the output also consistent (a range), if we change the process step or resource application level, the results would vary (un-predictable). So every successful organization wants the best process to be documented and used by their employees, so that they can repeat the success.

In normal life, most of us are following processes, but not all of them are written. When we live as in small family, we communicate the processes to others and ensure everybody follow the processes in life. However when it comes to an organization where unknown people work jointly to execute some work, this oral communication of process will not work in many cases and that's the reason we document the processes and make it available for everyone.

The simpler and effective way of writing a process is using ETVX method. E- Entry Criteria, T – Tasks, V- Validation criteria and X- Exit Criteria. This method will help in achieving clarity in writing processes. Similarly if we have a clearly developed workflow, that can help in reducing chaos.

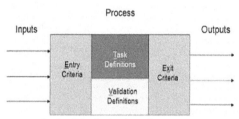

We will take for example the Technical review process,

Entry Criteria: New or Revised product ready for review

Tasks: Prepare for review, conduct review, record review comments, close the review comments

Validation: Review Report submission, Audits

Exit Criteria: Agreed review report

In addition to these Inputs and outputs, Roles performing the tasks will be mentioned and measures considered for the process.

The following can be the Process description details,

1 Objective

2 Scope

3 Entry Criteria

4 Acronyms and Abbreviations

5 Inputs

6 Process Descriptions

6.1 Activity 1

6.2 Activity 2

6.3 Activity 3

7 Recommendations

8 Permitted Tailoring

9 Measures

10 Validations

11 Quality Records

12 Exit Criteria

13 References (CMMI, Other Processes and Other Standards)

14 Process Profile Matrixes

Standard

Standards specify uniform use of specific technologies, parameters or procedures when such use will benefit the organization. Ex: Coding Standards

Guidelines

Guidelines assist users in implementing policies/ procedures, which may warrant variations, or which are under trials and imposition of standards is not always achievable. Ex: Estimation Guideline

Procedures

Procedures assist in complying with applicable policies, standards and guidelines. They are detailed steps to be followed by users to accomplish a particular task. Procedures may contain certain templates to be followed while executing the task.

Templates

They are prescribed format for creating documents/deliverables expected by the processes. A well defined template helps us in achieving consistency in capturing information and reduces the redundancy.

Earlier we have seen the sections of Quality Manual and process was given, they were nothing but templates. We can add the relevant details to make a document out of it.

Checklists

They help in gathering data in required manner and also not to miss out any relevant information, which also help us determine the occurrence of event.

Ex: Review Checklist, travel checklist and so on.

Documents in QMS:

Documents are key part in Quality Management System, as they are live in nature and kept updated to communicate the relevant information to the relevant groups in the organization. Documents are part of QMS, and documents are also part of projects or product development or any relevant activities. Documents have life and they undergo changes, primarily they are current and futuristic, and old documents are archived. To simply define the lifecycle of documents, we can say, create, review, release preparation, release & distribute, update and archive and retain.

In order to control the document in this lifecycle (traceable and easily detectable) it's important to assign version numbers and maintain the release details. Example of Documents can be a project plan, schedule, user manual, etc

Records are of special type of documents which conveys the information/data of a particular instance, simply a snap shot. Records are mostly used as evidence and they are not modifiable and they are documents which will undergo changes. Examples of records are attendance sheet, meeting minutes, training feedbacks, etc

In the past we used to have Master List of Document Control sheet as key document, which has the complete list of all documents and records, so that better control and traceability on documents were achieved at project level/functional level/organizational level. Now a day since we have many tools like share point and others, they simply create the master list and our job of manual maintaining them is reduced.

Master List of Document Control

Sl.No	Document Name	Document ID	Version No	Author	Distribution List	Path /Location
1	Quality Manual	JHF-MAN-QM-01	2.0	MR	Entire organization	Link
2						
3						
4						
5						
6						
7						
8						
9						

Master List of Records Control

Sl.No	Record Name	Document ID	Author	Custodian	Record Media Type	Retention Period	Path /Location
1	Fault Log			IT	Soft Copy	3 Years	Link
2							

3							
4							
5							

A Quality Management System contains in addition to these items, Roles and Responsibility document. Which is actually describes which roles are performing what activities in the organization.

In addition to these the Quality Management system may contain repositories. They are nothing but useful information derived from projects which are available for the new projects to refer. Past estimations, plans, samples, defects and so on can be collected from projects and categorized and cleansed and added as part of repositories. They help for the new projects to understand quickly from others data or learning.

The following are the typical repositories maintained in organizations,

     (i)   Measurement Repository

     (ii)   Estimation Repository

     (iii)   Defect Repository

     (iv)   Service issues Repository

     (v)   Risk Repository

     (vi)   Lifecycle Repository

     (vii) Tailoring Repository

(viii) Best Practices Repository

(ix) Lessons Learnt Repository

(x) Samples Repository

(xi) Technical Know How – FAQ's

And other different repositories like reusable repository, domain specific repositories, etc

Every repository may have an identified person allocated to maintain it. The data cleansing activity is performed, before adding the data to a repository. Adequate Communication in this regard will help in better utilization. Some organizations use share point or web portal to publish their repositories, and hit counters are enabled to check how many clicks to the portal happened for the repository.

QMS Benefits:

- Quality Management System helps an organization to perform effectively.

- It helps the Organization to deliver Quality Product/Service.

- Projects are handled systematically and project deliveries are controlled

- It increases the employee confidence in performing a task.

- It ensures systematic way of handling changes and applying innovative technologies.

- Process stability and capability is improved in the organization

- Improves reusability of components in the organization

- Reduction in cost of the product development/service delivery

- Improvement in delivery cycle time and time to market

2 QUALITY ASSURANCE FUNCTIONS

Quality Assurance (QA) activities as we discussed earlier are the one which gives confidence to the organization and to client that by following the Quality Management System the final product or services will be of quality. It may not be possible to get the quality product/services as soon as we define set of processes, templates, roles and responsibilities, etc (QMS) it may need few iterations to learn that what's working for you and what's not. Most of the times, the system is improved by getting feedback continuously from the Operational teams and by measuring the process capability. Based on the feedback and improvement opportunities the processes and system components will be updated by the identified teams. These new updated/revised processes in the system are implemented by Operational teams and again they are measured and feedback is collected. The system is updated or revised till the expected quality is achieved. In order to perform this cycle (its similar to PDCA) we need different Quality Assurance functions to act in the system. The following are some of the key functions within QA,

Software Engineering Process Group (SEPG):

The group consists of Subject Matter Experts from various engineering and management areas and Process quality assurance members/ Software Quality Analysts. Few of the SME's can be permanent members and few can work on need basis (depending on how often their process is discussed). Typically each SME is identified with relevant processes in mind. The Process Quality Assurance Members who are contributing in process definition and who are performing facilitation & audits shall represent. This helps in getting real issues from the ground and discusses with SME and put it in presentable process format.

- SEPG is responsible for Process Focus and alignment with business objectives

- SEPG ensures that relevant processes are defined to support the delivery

- SEPG ensures that process assets are created and maintained

- SEPG makes deployment and process action plans

- Process revision and maintenance is taken care by them

- Process tailoring and relevant analysis is performed

- Process Improvements achievement and sources maintenance

- SEPG is responsible for process appraisals

- SEPG is responsible for overall Quality Management System development and deployment

Process Quality Assurance/ Software Quality Analyst Group:

This group consists of people who has competency on process quality assurance. Typically it includes people who can understand the process architecture, its application and improvement needs. Process compliance activities like QA reviews and Process compliance audits are performed by them. Independency and objectivity should be maintained on forming this group.

- Project facilitation and hand holding on Process implementation

- Process training performed by them

- Product Quality Assurance review performed

- Process Compliance Audits are performed

- Project level metrics analysis support

- Tailoring of processes are supported

- Interact with SEPG, project teams and metrics team to provide relevant updates

- Some organizations use them for Risk Assessment or other security compliance standards implementation.

Metrics Analyst Group:

This group consists of people who have understanding on project management, statistics and process control. Their ability to understand the data and process is important to do further analysis. The project management understanding is more of logical understanding of project's phases and actual condition. The analysis and reporting shall be meaningful for the project and organization to use it for informed decision making. This group may not exist in all organizations as separate group and may be available wherever high volume of data is there and criticality of data analysis for decision making is high.

Audit Group:

In some organizations separate audit groups are formed and they may be in addition to the audits performed by Software Quality Analysts (SQA) or at corporate level auditing on few critical accounts. Typically trained auditor with multiple models and standards knowledge is part of the team.

Process Consultancy:

Few organizations deliver Software Process consultancy services with their SQA team. The members in the team are chosen based on the experience in handling clients and potential to solve problems. Typically the services can be to the local market or to the International market and also it may be for existing clients or for new clients. The team shall be having separate delivery model and pricing model to attract the clients and deliver services. In this case, the SQA team is no longer a support team, but revenue generating operational team.

Characteristic of a good SQA:

The SQA can be part of any of the mentioned teams, though it's expected he is part of the process QA group and facilitate the projects. However if the SQA has experience in all the relevant roles then it's an added advantage for the Organization. For an SQA to be successful the following are the key characteristics he/she should have,

- ✓ Good Listening Ability

- ✓ Ability to visualize and form the problem statement

- ✓ Ability to visualize solution and its modifications over a period of time

- ✓ Believing every complex problem has simple solutions

- ✓ Ability to find multiple solutions

- ✓ Ability to separate emotions, process, people in a given context

- ✓ Fact finding ability

- ✓ Less distraction from the goal

- ✓ Ready to accept mistakes and stand firm on decisions

- ✓ Establish Objectivity and be non biased

- ✓ Analyze a problem from process point of view and from people point of view

- ✓ Risk based evaluations should be the goal

- ✓ Understand client needs and business models

- ✓ Think like senior management and bring solutions with larger perspective

- ✓ Concentration on prevention and on addressing root causes

3 LIFECYCLE MODELS

A Software is developed using distinct phases and they are arranged in a manner that the product can be produced on time with quality. This arrangement of phases to deliver product/service is called lifecycle. There are lifecycles with pre-arranged phases and each of them having their own controls is available, and they are commonly used in organizations. Lifecycles tend to declare the way the development/service related activities will be executed in a project. The phases in a lifecycle, has clear objective to achieve, has clear tasks and performed in time period (time period block). The phases are customizable and can be defined on our own to suit our development/services. Similarly the lifecycles are customizable and can be defined on our own with arrangements of phases.

Lifecycle becomes important to communicate the way we are going to develop the product to every stakeholders and what to expect and when, becomes clearer with this.

Some of the basic standard lifecycles are,

- Waterfall Model

- Incremental Model

- V Model

- Iterative Model

And there are many other models available commercially to use. However many of them are customized version of these base models and sometime with Risk Evaluation of progressing with project. In addition, if we work with maintenance project then we have maintenance lifecycle, Business Intelligence, Migration, conversion projects and so on has their own lifecycles. Be clear, when we know what we want to produce and what are the key steps, how important for us to validate the product early in its development (internally/client), etc can help us to customize or develop our own models. So we would leave it to you to customize the lifecycle model or select some of the commercially available model for your product development/service delivery.

Waterfall Model:

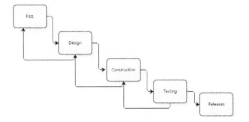

The simplest method used in software development is this waterfall model. The phases have clear sequence and no overlaps. The initial phase starts with Requirements phases, where at the end of the phase the requirements documents are produced and signed off, and then in subsequent design phase the design related activities are executed and design documents are created and signed off. In construction phase, coding and unit testing is performed. In Testing phase test execution is performed on the product and finally the product gets released in release phase.

Salient Points -

- Clear Distinctive phases

- Simpler flow

- Any change requested by client in the middle phases, has to go through the previous phases

- End of each phase produces baselined documents/work products

- Requirements are frozen in this model at the beginning itself, however in normal life, the requirements are more of evolving in nature or client keep adding few to ensure product is of current and useful in nature

- Long duration projects is not suitable for this type, considering lot of apprehension will be created in client and development team mind, as they see the executable software only in the last period of development.

Incremental Model:

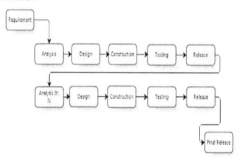

The core requirements are collected in the Initial stage. The requirements are realized as product in multiple incremental cycles by splitting the requirements in to relevant modules/blocks which can produce workable software, and which can be deployed. Every incremental cycle adds additional feature to the product and before the final release the product is tested in complete and released.

For example if a bank wants to provide banking services through ATM, they may go on developing the software with multiple increments and initially with few basic features to launch with (withdrawal & account statement), then they keep adding new features (loan request, change of client address, etc).

Salient features

- Each Increment produces useful software

- Each Increment is having additional features, which are planned

- Each Increment also addresses deficiencies identified in previous cycle

- Client can see the product features in defined timeline

- Changes can be accommodated in the same cycle or in the next cycle

This lifecycle is commonly used as structured lifecycle. If we notice the waterfall model is followed in each increment in this case. Instead we can apply V model in each increment or any other base model on each increment. That will give customized lifecycle.

V Model:

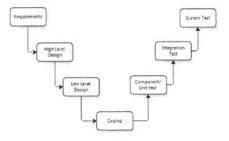

By the shape it looks like the alphabet "V", so it's referred as V model. Don't ask, why can't it can be kept flat and why as "V". The justifying point is, each phases from requirements till coding has their own testing phases (unit test to system test) to test the deliverable. Similarly it represents Verification and Validation activities. This V model is what most of us use in practical life. However we customize this model, by adding it inside another model or in a cycle. The model brings in the clarity on testing activities and well defined testing practices, helps us to produce better quality product.

Requirements are tested with System tests, High Level design is tested with Integration tests, and similarly the code and low level design components are tested with Unit testing. This is practical because in the requirements phases itself the testing preparation starts.

Salient points

- Better Product testing methodology

- Clear phases and covers all the engineering basics

- Each phase contributes to further downstream phases

- In multivendor environment, where different teams work on different parts of lifecycle, this is very useful model

- Better defect prevention and control activities can be exercised.

As we discussed earlier it represents Verification and Validation activities, let's see what they are,

Verification:

Simple Definition: It checks, "Are we building the product right?"

Verification is an activity which ensures that product development is as per the standards and goals in a phase. Basically we check the conformance to requirements.

For example, you want to go from Mumbai (India) to Columbus (US), and you have to take three flights Mumbai to London, London to New York, New York to Columbus. Let's see what verification in this journey is.

From Mumbai when you reach London, you check whether you have collected/taken your relevant articles, if there any form to submit in airport did you fill it and you have all relevant details (ticket/accessories) to board the next flight. All these activities are only verifying whether you have reached the place as per plan and followed the guidance/standard to reach there and ready for next phase.

Validation:

Simple Definition: It checks, "Are we building the right product?"

Validation is an activity which ensures that product development is as per the goal and intent of the project/program. We keep checking at every phase, the fitness of the product for purpose.

In our example, when we reach London, we check the path and time to see whether we will be able to reach Columbus on time. If we believe we are already late/early, we might be asking for alternate flights to reach the place. In validation we check for the final goal.

What it means is, we keep doing Verification and Validation together in most of the cases, however knowledge on what is verification and what is validation, will help in better planning and execution. In software development, Verification is primarily performed with techniques like reviews, inspections and walkthrough, etc Validation is performed using testing, prototype and client validation, etc

Iterative Model:

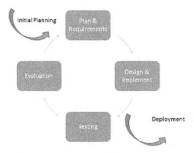

The product is developed with number of iterations. The initial iteration concentrating on the critical features of the product, the subsequent iterations add/modify or correct the features and get deployed for taking the feedback. This model is good when we have a product where the requirements are unclear and the outcome needs good amount of involvement of client and development team has to experiment few things. The phases are arranged in a manner, that evaluation of the software is one of the critical phases to progress or to continue the project. This model considers the Risk Evaluation in iterations for better planning and execution of the product development. This model is used along with Incremental model in many circumstances.

Salient features:

- Product features can be evaluated quickly.

- Project team gets quick feedback and the level of confidence increases

- Requirements clarity increases

- It can become uncontrollable if not managed with clear expectations, as iterations could lead to surprise additions.

Apart from these models, we have Rational Unified Process (RUP), Prototype, Spiral and so many other lifecycle models are available. However as we described earlier lifecycle models can be customized and created, and it needs basic understanding on the phases and output we need at the end of each phase and clear purpose on what we want to achieve. Risk evaluation phase addition in any model will benefit, however it depends on the need and cost of development.

Some basics for Customizing/creating lifecycles

- Clear Phases identified

- Each phase has clear deliverables and actions identified in it

- Interrelationship between different phases are explained

- Sequence or arrangement of phases to execute product development/Service delivery is documented

- Client involvement level/need to be considered on designing the lifecycle

- Requirements Change Risks to be considered

- Need of evaluation and Research activities, to be considered in designing the lifecycle

- Milestones, sign offs and delivery payments to be considered

- Each phase to be value addition to the product development/service delivery

- Lifecycle should be able to build confidence on product quality (Verification & Validation) considerations.

And other key features required for the relevant context to be considered appropriately.

4 PROJECT MANAGEMENT

A Project is a temporary activity to develop a product or deliver a service and which has definite start and end. We too have projects in life, our schooling; internships, job and sometimes people consider marriage also as project. It's always confusing that we keep listening to the words projects, program and products. There are many definitions available for them in Project Management Body of Knowledge (PMI) and in ISO standards. However for our simpler understanding, Projects has clear start and end timeline and normally we expect it to contain marginal volume of work to execute and deliver product or service. A program can comprise of many projects, whereas the program is large and continuous in nature. The complexities in a program could be higher and a significant change in the resultant environment is expected due to a program. Product is an outcome of project and/or program. The product development companies have product level lifecycle and product level plan, and multiple projects can be part of making the product level plan succeed.

Project Management is application of knowledge, skills, tools and techniques to project activities in order to meet the project goals and requirements. Its managing the dependencies, resources for achieving the target/developing product/delivering services as planned.

Every project has assigned Project Manager, who handles the Project Management. For a Software Quality Analyst it's important to understand the project management and to be able to think in line with project manager. We would recommend that the SQA is in par with the Project manager.

Project Management has the following Phases:

Project planning to start with, Project Monitoring and control and then Project closure

Project Planning:

Purpose of this phase is to devise a plan and get commitment from all the stakeholders towards the plan.

- This is the initial phase in Project Management, some organizations has Initiation as separate phase before this.

- Scope of work/Contractual terms are understood

- Estimations on Schedule, Effort and Cost is performed

- Commitment on deliveries and goals are made from project managers/delivery heads

- Project resources are identified for successful delivery

- Project Organization is formed and responsibilities allocated

- Risks and dependencies are identified and tracked

- Create a Project plan which integrates all other sub plans of execution

- Get commitment from internal and external stakeholders on the plan

Project Monitoring and Control:

Purpose of this phase is to monitor the progress of project and track the actual parameters and deliverables, and controls the parameters to achieve success in the project.

- Monitor the Effort and schedule along with deliveries

- Monitor the risks and issues in the project

- Monitor the team motivation and utilization

- Monitor the deliverable quality and productivity

- Monitor the commitments are being met by all stakeholders

- Control the variations in Effort/Schedule/Cost and other identified parameters

- Monitor the contractual clauses and scope of work commitments

- Update the plan as per scope changes (if any) with adequate impact analysis

- Ensure the communication flow with relevant stakeholders

- Escalate as required to the relevant members

- Ensure the deliveries are met as per the commitment

Project closure:

This is the final phase of project management, where a complete understanding on how the project was performed and final settlement of activities are performed, so that the project can be formally closed in an organization.

- Project financial settlements are closed

- Client sign off is obtained

- All relevant information pertaining to project is archived

- Information useful for other projects are shared with QA function

- Project Closure report is prepared

- Stakeholders are communicated with project closure details.

- Lesson learnt documents are prepared.

And other internal expectations are met.

Project Plan:

Project Management as we discussed earlier has many activities to be performed, however the key activity is project plan preparation. Most of the activities we mentioned here, either contributes to preparation of this document or revolves around tracking and executing project as per this document.

So what is a project plan and why it's required?

Project plan is a complete roadmap for realizing your project. It contains all the relevant information from your contract to lifecycle to resources to communication and schedule, etc. This is the complete realization plan based on which project will be executed.

If you are asked to develop a single page web application with just a screen with information and you are the only one, who is going to work, I don't think you need a project plan. However if you are given with a web page development with various functional details of a school and you and your friend is going to work, may be you both need at least a schedule to work on. In case you have to develop an interactive web page for an educational institute and 20 people are working than, you may need a plan to better describe the way the responsibilities will be shared and timelines more clearly. In case the same is with 100 people, do we think, we can manage everyone without a plan and clarity in communications? We definitely need a plan.

In the event of making a project plan, in fact many things will become clear for the project manager and team.

A project plan consists of following elements,

a) Introduction

Purpose

<Describe the purpose of the document>

Scope

<Describe what is in the scope and what is not in the scope of the document>

Abbreviations and Acronyms

<List the abbreviations and acronyms available in the document>

Definitions

<List the definitions which require explanation for better understanding in the document>

References

<Describe the documents / work products that are referred to develop this document>

b) Project Profile

Project Name:

Client Name and Contact Details:

Project billing type:

Domain:

Technology:

Start Date:

End Date:

Project Overview:

Project Scope:

Project Objectives and Goals:

Assumptions and Constraints:

c) Project Environment

Environment Details	
Hardware	
Operating System	
Compiler	
Interfacing Hardware/Software	

d) Lifecycle Model, Phases & Deliverables

<Insert Lifecycle model flow>

Project Phases	Deliverables

e) Work Break Down Structure with Schedule

<Link Excel or .mpp or other file format specifying the tasks and schedule>

f) User Acceptance Criteria

g) Project Estimation

<Provide a link to the Project's Estimation worksheets / artifacts>

h) Resource Plan

Hardware

<Include the number of servers, test machines, shared machines, desktops/laptops or any other special hardware like switches, routers that may be required by the team.>

Description	Configuration/ Specification	Quantity Required	Start Date	End date
Hardware \<Name>				
Software \<Name>				
Others \<Name>				

Competency Evaluation and Training Plan

\<Link to resource Competency evaluation sheet and also identify the trainings accordingly>

Human Resource Plan

S.No	Name of the Resource	Role	% Involvement	Start Date	End Date
1					
2					
3					
4					
5					

Project Organization

\<Graphically indicate below the project team structure >

Roles & Responsibilities

Role	Responsibilities

i) Stakeholders and Dependencies

<Document the project's internal and external dependencies >

Stakeholders	Dependency Description	Lifecycle Phase	Required by (Date)

j) Risk and Issue Management

<Provide Link to Risk Management log & Issue log >

k) Configuration Management and Change Management

<Provide link to the Configuration Management Plan with Change Management details>

l) Communication Plan

Information required	Stakeholder/s	When (phase/frequency)	Purpose
Weekly Report			
Monthly Report			
Others			

m) Verification and Validation

\<List Reviews and Link to Test Plan/strategy>

n) Project Tracking Plan

Tracking Mode	Frequency	Participants
Project progress review		
Project Monitoring Review		
Milestone Review		
Client review		
Others		

o) Quality Management

\<Provide link to the Quality Plan or Schedule with activities>

Process Planning

\<Use Tailoring Sheet to plan for the processes>

p) Other Plans

\<Indicate other plans like Product integration plan, installation plan, training plan for users, etc here>.

q) Warranty Support

\<Indicate the Warranty period, and terms of Warranty support >

Key elements in this plan:

The following are the key components we would like to verify or ensure,

- The scope of work should be as per contractual terms

- Dependencies with client should be clear and it should not be part of assumptions

- Assumptions documented here, should not be ambiguous in nature

- Work Break down Structure to have tasks which are less than 4 man days duration as far as possible for better controlling

- Usage of Gantt chart helps in scheduling and scheduling to have dependencies of tasks and resource allocation affiliated with it.

- Estimation with proven techniques helps in managing the project with realistic goals

- Resources and their roles, responsibilities allocation in formal manner helps in evaluation and better clarity in reporting and action completion.

- The support plans like Quality plan, test plan, risk plan, configuration plan and other plans helps to ensure the dates are in sync, no role clashes, dependencies are clear, etc. Some organizations calls this as integrated project plan, as all other plans are integrated with this one plan.

- Milestones are identified clearly, which is a specific point in time in a project, where important deliverables or good amounts of days are spent. This is a specific point, where organization and client may be interested to look back at the project progress, evaluate and plan/re-plan for future course.

- Warranty period has to be understood and the plan should cover it.

- Issue management and escalation management are key areas in project management, where identification and tracking of them can be like science; however bringing actions to close them is more of an art, as we are dealing with client or key stakeholders.

- A project manager is not a machine and project plan is not manufacturing plan fed in to a machine, its management, which needs application of knowledge in the right context and at right time. There is good amount of judgment involved and great amount of people emotions involved. A project manager should be aware of all the project management techniques and knowledge areas to be a better informed person, and he can use the relevant techniques to derive solutions, however the logic and people value consideration and application of certain solution in certain context is still an art.

- Risk management is important for better project management. If you keep identifying and tracking and closing risks with respect to your project, nearly you will achieve half success with it.

The project plan is revised whenever there is deviation found from current state and the planned state, also whenever the future state is going to change from what was planned earlier. The project plan has to be kept up to date, as this the plan everyone is following. It's like keeping the road signals up to date, if the road is blocked, but your signal says you can travel in the road, it will only create confusion.

However when smaller teams work and less complex activities are performed, the project teams just jump in to requirements and coding. In this case, even design takes less priority, so we expecting a detailed plan are just a dream. Hence organizations come out with small project plan templates, and in some other cases, they just ask a Gantt chart of schedule to proceed with.

What an SQA can check:

- Check the Scope of work and Contractual terms documented in plan

- Check the acceptance criteria

- Check the estimations and schedule with standard methods and details

- Check the Lifecycle phases and deliverables clarity

- Check the project organization structure

- Check the reporting methods and communications

- In addition check the project plan template and process planning and all sections in project plan for completeness

- Check if the project plan is reviewed internally and comments are captured

- Check if the project plan is approved

- Check Project meetings are happening and actions captured and tracked to closure

- Check the Minutes of meeting, Status report and other relevant records

- Check the Metrics report of the projects and how project is progressing

- Check the schedule and effort is kept up to date and all the changes in scope is captured and the plan is revised accordingly

- Check the competency evaluation of team and trainings they have undergone.

- Check project closure report is produced

The points given here are some of the key points; however they are not comprehensive in nature. Every organization normally has work product review checklist for SQA activities and they have to follow them to check the project plan and related execution.

5 CONFIGURATION MANAGEMENT

Configuration Management is identifying and managing the configurable items to support integrity in delivery of service or product. Configuration management is critical in product development and in complex deliveries. Sometimes there is very low attention is paid to this area and those results in wrong build, failure in installation, etc. Configuration Management sometimes looked only along with release, however configuration management starts from the beginning of a project till the product is deployed and maintained.

It involves activities like configurable items identification, setting up of configuration control board, Baseline the configurable items, manage the change requests, apply changes, and perform status accounting and Configuration Audits. In addition to this, naming convention and backup and retrieval are also important activities in configuration management.

Configurable item: Any component which is part of the product development, and a change in the product without adequate control can have negative impact to the product development/project, and then the item is a configurable item and should be identified and tracked. This includes planning elements, logs, code and all other relevant items.

A laptop has so many components and if we change one component and put in some other one which is available in your house, will it work? Hopefully we will not do this; instead we will check the current configuration, serial number, version of the component and will replace it with a compatible component. Similarly in a project you can't have a wrong project plan, wrong source code or wrong MOM; in fact all these are configurable items.

Configuration Control Board: This is team of identified members who has the authority to evaluate any new change proposal (request) and decide on approval or rejection. They understand the business, time, context and change impact, etc to decide on the change request.

Configuration System: It involves tools/directories, method and resources to handle configurable items and manage them. Ex: SVN/CVS/VSS and so on, along with procedures

Naming Conventions and Versioning: Each configurable item is assigned with unique naming. Normally this is defined by organization or client given guideline is followed. We can decide based on the project name, department name, category of document, name of document and based on that we can generate 3 letter short conventions to make a label.

XXX-YYY-ZZZ- 1.0

XXX- project name

YYY- Category of item

ZZZ- name of document

What is 1.0 here?

This is the versioning part of the Configurable item. As the document will undergo changes, having a naming convention will only help us separate the document from one another, but not between its own versions.

Typically we follow,

0.1 – draft version

0.2 – updated draft version, and 0.3, 0.4 like that for all draft versions

1.0 – Release version

1.1 – Revised version for minor change (Increase by 0.1 for minor changes)

2.0 – Revised Release version (for major changes increase it to next full digit)

However for product developments they normally use three or four digit versioning, like 1.0.0 or 1.0.0.0

Sometimes organizations use few tools for managing configurations, which has the ability to provide internal versioning number and manages them. So the organizations don't use additional versioning in the document. In such a case, it's important to give the changes details when they save the document for each new version and also to perform frequent configuration audits to ensure that the current documents are uploaded in to the Configuration system.

In case of documents, it's a normal practice for organizations to update the versioning and naming convention in Header/Footer of document and similarly the revision details in the document's first few pages or in last page, with details on what is revised and when.

Configuration Manager/Controller: This person is responsible for managing configurable items and relevant configurations for each release. This person also needs to perform the status accounting and managing the changes. Every project shall have this role identified.

Baseline of Configurable Item: A baseline point is critical to quality an identified configurable item as part of a baseline. This ensures that the configurable items are available for use and that's the one, everybody should refer. For example, a project plan is identified as configurable item, but when everybody will start using or referring is when it's baselined. A baseline point for Project plan is it's approved internally by the delivery management. Once the plan is approved it will be moved to the baseline folder, hence from now onwards, everyone will be referring this plan as baseline plan to work. Any further changes to this plan can't be done arbitrarily, it has to follow change management procedure and the new baseline has to be informed to relevant stakeholders.

Change management:

Change Requests: This is of two types, one coming from client and could be mainly on scope of work related changes (addition/modification/etc) and another one coming from internally, this could be either change in scope/product/service which we want to evaluate and apply along with client or change in internal documents as part of development. In all the cases, the change requests are raised and depending upon the type of change requests (standard/minor/major) it's sent to configuration control board for evaluation.

Impact Analysis: Almost all the change requests undergo impact analysis, where the different components which will get impacted and effort/schedule involved and context and timing of change is evaluated. When its standard change requests which has predefined path and pre approved, then impact analysis don't play role there. These impact analysis reports are used by Configuration control board for further decision making.

Change Implementation: The approved changes are taken for implementation and the relevant components are updated. As required by the change, the components may be tested or evaluated with other methods. On successful validation of changes the relevant stakeholders are informed.

All the change requests are tracked using a change request log with the current state of progress and it's updated and maintained.

Status Accounting:

At any given point in time, the statuses of configurable items are taken as snapshot. This includes taking the current description of configurable items from your tool (in olden days Master list of documents and records used to support this), Status of change requests, status of items which are in the process of change implementation. A combination of these will actually gives the status accounting in a particular point in time. This activity is repeated at frequent intervals or based on the need. This is critical, as any point in time, if you want to restore back to a working condition of your product, it's possible with status accounting.

When Windows operating system crashes the restoration happens to a previous date, which is available, when the OS was working. This is nothing but the status accounting records available for that period and version of those files available, so Windows goes back to that point in time working software.

Configuration Auditing:

Configuration Audits help in ensuring that relevant versions are included in the right baselines and the system is ready for release with right configurations. Configuration Audit consists of physical and functional configuration audits. The purpose of physical configuration audit is to ensure that relevant configurable item is available with the right details and in right baseline/build. In Functional configuration audit the purpose is to ensure that the right content is available in the configurable item and completeness of the configurable item. These both ensure the integrity of the final release.

If you buy a television and you see a user manual of DVD player or you found the user manual of TV, but the contents are for some other series TV of that brand, or you find the sections are misarranged with their titles, it means there was no Configuration Audit conducted in it.

Configuration Plan includes the following,

1.0 Overview
      1.1 Purpose
      1.2 Scope
2.0 Configuration Management System
      2.1 Roles and Responsibilities
      2.2 Resources & Tools
      2.3 Naming Convention for CIs
      2.4 CM Repository Structure
      2.5 Interface with other Teams
3.0 Configuration Identification and Baseline details

      3.1 Baselines

SL#	Baseline	Purpose & Point of	Contents

		Baseline	

3.2 Configuration Items

SL#	CI ID	CI Name	Approved By	Baseline Details

4.0 Change Management and Release
    4.1 Access Control Rights
    4.2 Change Request tracking
    4.3 Change Control procedure
    4.4 Versioning
    4.5 Back and Restore
    4.6 Interface with build or Product Integration plan reference
    4.7 Release and Numbering
5.0 Status Accounting and Configuration Auditing
    5.1 Status Accounting
    5.2 Configuration Auditing

Configuration Management Benefits:

- Better tracking of changes

- Clarity in outputs and management

- Supportive to better release management

- Reduction in redundancy issues

- Management of baselines and its components

- Supports complex development environments

- Support continuous builds

- Supports in distributed working team models to manage the configurations.

6 SOFTWARE ESTIMATION

Estimation in software industry is an area where lots been experimented and there are few methods available with us to do better estimation compared 15 years or so. In our normal life we do estimation regular basis without much problem, like we estimate our arrival time, we estimate height, size, weight and so many. But how do we do, mostly it's based on past experiences and some extrapolation, addition of buffer to counteract unknown characteristics.

In software Estimation we mainly concentrate on estimating Size, effort, cost and schedule. The estimations are performed in various instances like,

- Proposal stage

- Project planning stage

- Requirements stage

- Design Stage

- Whenever Change in scope happens

The estimation flow could be broadly put in this way,

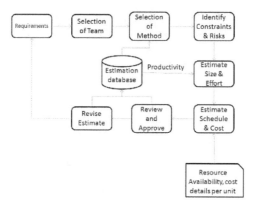

We will see some of the estimation methods which are used in industry commonly,

Three point Estimation:

In this method the estimations are based on three different values for any given context. The pessimistic, optimistic and most likely values are the three different values considered in this method. Effort is directly calculated using this method without any size. This method is used in some organizations where the estimation has lesser role (smaller projects/tasks). Experience of the members estimating, plays key role in the success of estimation in this method. However in some cases this method is used for Size calculation based on LOC for the programs and the final derived Size is multiplied with productivity to derive effort.

Estimation value= (Optimistic value+ pessimistic value + 4* (most likely value))/ 6

Wide Band Delphi:

This another method based on expertise in an activity, in this method also the effort is directly derived and no size calculation. In this method, the experts are called and explained the requirements and related contexts, and they are asked to provide their estimation separately without any discussion with others.

The estimations are plotted and the lowest and highest values are declared and rationale for them is understood from the members. In a session the context and available more details are provided to the members, and again they are asked to estimate. In this way at some point, the values are closer and that based on consensus that estimates is taken for further usage.

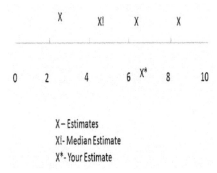

X – Estimates
XI - Median Estimate
X* - Your Estimate

Standard Components Method:

In this method, based on overall scope of work, the different components which have to be produced are listed down. There are rules created to identify the components with certain level of complexity. Based on the rules, every component (based on type) is assigned with certain complexity. Normally the components are classified as like simple, medium and complex. The effort allocation is based on their complexity value. It's more of relative effort allocation, as the simple component takes some X hours, the medium component may take 1.5* X hours in that way its allocated. The Effort in this method is calculated mainly for construction phase using the components; hence the effort has to be extrapolated to cover other phases in development (Requirement, design, testing, etc) and overall development effort derived. With this the additional effort for project management, quality assurance, configuration management, buffer effort, etc are added to derive the final effort. This method is mostly adopted in many organizations as usual method. However not having a size value, makes this method weak. The comparison with other projects is not possible, because the size of the product is unknown. However it's simple and effective in many contexts, as long as the team follows the rules clearly.

In this same method, few organizations add weightage based on, simple work equivalent to 1 unit of size (1 day effort) and as the complexity increases the unit also allocated with higher weightage, and the total is calculated as Unit of Work. They use this value as Size.

Components

	Simple	Medium	Complex	Very Complex
Screens	2	3	4	5
Reports	4	4	3	3
Tables	3	2	2	10
Procedures	5	4	1	2

Effort Table

	Simple	Medium	Complex	Very Complex
Screens	10	20	30	60
Reports	15	30	60	80
Tables	20	40	80	90
Procedures	25	50	90	120

Effort Ratio Table- To Build weightage

	Simple	Medium	Complex	Very Complex
Screens	1	2	3	6
Reports	1.5	3	6	8
Tables	2	4	8	9
Procedures	2.5	3	9	12

Development Sizing using effort ratio table

	Simple	Medium	Complex	Very Complex	
Screens	2*1	3*2	4*3	5*6	50
Reports	4*1.5	4*3	3*6	3*8	54
Tables	3*2	2*4	2*8	10*9	128
Procedures	5*2.5	4*5	1*9	2*12	65.5
				Total development Points (Size)	289.5

Smallest unit Effort is 10 hrs   Total Development effort   2895

SDLC Phase		Normal step	
	Req	15%	108.56
	Des	20%	144.75
	Cod	40%	289.5
	Tes	20%	144.75
	Build	5%	36.18
		Total SDLC Effort	723.74

Other Effort			
	PM	10% of(SDLC)	72.3
	CM	5% of (SDLC)	36.18
	QM	3% of (SDLC)	21.71
	DM	5% of (SDLC)	36.18
	Buffer	5% of (SDLC)	36.18
		Total Other effor	202.55

	Total Project Effort		926.29
	Development Size		289.5

Function Point Method:

This method is one of the most used methods in estimation. This is basically a measurement method for sizing; however this is used in the early stages of the project, with the available requirements and features details. The Size calculation is getting refined over a period as there is clarity in requirements and in features. This size measuring method was published first by A J Albrecht of IBM. Currently this method is owned by International Function Point User Group (IFPUG) and they have brought in few changes to cope with newer technologies and type of projects.

Function points measure the functionality delivered by an application from the user's perspective.

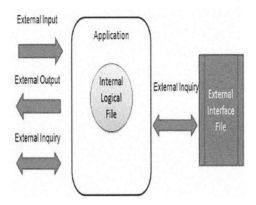

In Function point calculation we need to fix the boundary of the application first. What is included, excluded, data accessed from other applications, interface with hardware, etc are identified and boundary is fixed.

The functionality is classified as External Input (Processing data or control information which enters in to the application boundary), External Output(Processed data or information that exits the application boundary), External Inquiry (Process retrieves data from the application boundary with request), Internal Logical File (User identifiable group of logically related data maintained within the application boundary) and External Interface File (User identifiable group of logically related data used within the application boundary, but maintained by external application/ interfaces).

The different functionalities are identified under these categories and listed. Each of them are classified for their complexity, based on the record/files and data elements they handle and they are classified as Low, Average, High complexities (pre fixed tables with values based on tables helps to find the complexities). Then they are converted in to function point count using the weightage based on complexities. The table with weights for all five types of functionalities is available (pre-defined)

Function Type	Low	Average	High
EI	x 3	x 4	x 6
EO	x 4	x 5	x 7
EQ	x 3	x 4	x 6
ILF	x 7	x 10	x 15
EIF	x 5	x 7	x 10

Multiplying the number of functionalities with relevant weightage gives Unadjusted Function point count.

However few organizations use the 14 General system characteristics (like data communication, performance, online data entry, etc) and apply the influence level (0 to 5 scales), to bring a value which is called Variable Adjustment Factor (VAF). The count of total influences are calculated by adding the influences degree, this value can be minimum 0 to maximum 70 (the reason is 14 times of 5).

Adjusted Function Points are derived using = Unadjusted Function Point count * VAF

Whereas VAF = 0.65 + (0.01* Total Degree of Influence)

What it means is VAF can be on the lower side 0.65 and higher side 1.35 and can be any value in between. So if the unadjusted function point is 100, then based on VAF, the adjusted function point can vary between values 65 to 135.

In addition to these estimation methodologies there are cosmic function point method, Use case point estimation, feature point estimation and other methods are available. These methods are useful in estimating size and from there the effort is calculated.

In CosmicFP method they use Read, Write, and Entry and Exit type of data movement and before that the functional processes and sub processes are identified. This method is more useful in multi tier architecture environment.

Without size when we derive effort, we lose the advantage of comparison with other projects and also we will not able to calculate the productivity. As Productivity is something which is derived by comparing the Size produced with effort consumed, the case when we don't have productivity, further analysis and improvement becomes difficult. Whenever a method gives size, the effort is derived based on the past benchmarked productivity value in the organization (by multiplying) to derive the effort.

Sometimes organizations compare the estimated effort with actual effort and claim that as productivity, which is actually not. We may say that's an estimation index value which help as to compare plan with actual. However such metrics always brings inaccuracy, as we may do wrong estimation, or poor performance. Hence we can't clearly attribute these kinds of metrics.

Once the effort estimates are derived from Size or through direct methods, then we identify the resources and count, which will help us to fix the schedule. The resources are selected considering what could be the optimum size and lifecycle, etc, so that timelines can be met for the deliverables. Cost estimations are derived by using the resource cost and infrastructure cost and contribution margin/profit margins and total cost is derived.

7 RISK AND ISSUE MANAGEMENT

Risk Management

Risks are uncertainties in a project, which could negatively impact the project. Risk management is a formal activity which consists of Risk identification, Evaluation and implementation of action plans. Risk management in a project is the responsibility of project manager. Organizations may have Risk Management strategy devised at organizational level to guide the project manager.

Risk Identification – Risk Identification should be normally performed along with the team and usage of risk identification checklist and looking at past similar project's risk log, would help in identifying risks. Identified risks are normally tagged with category and source. These help to analyze the risks and to build risk repository.

Risk Evaluation – Risks are analyzed and evaluated. The probability and Severity of impact are judged (can have certain guidance at organizational level) and from that Risk Exposure Index is calculated. Probability tells us, the chance of risk happening in our project (a scale of 0 to 1 is used; sometimes customized scales are also used). Severity of Impact tells us, how bad the project can get impacted; if that happens (a scale of 1 to 5 or any customized value can be used). Risk Exposure Index is a multiplication of these two values,

Risk Exposure Index= Probability of occurrence * severity of impact

Based on the final Risk Exposure Index of identified Risks they are targeted for Risk treatment. In addition to this risk priority (timely response) is also evaluated, as some risks need to be addressed immediately and others could be little later, though their risk exposure value is high.

Risk Strategies:

The following are different ways of managing risks,

Risk Avoidance: Ensure that risks don't appear, by refraining/changing a task. For example, change in contract to avoid risk or not undertaking a work/exclusion from scope

Risk Mitigation: Take actions to reduce the impact or probability of risk. For example, Lack of knowledge in a domain, is mitigated with Knowledge transfer from a subject matter expert. When the risk mitigation fails to reduce the impact or probability, then risk contingency plan should be there to treat the risk. For example, in this same case when there is no improvement in knowledge, recruiting a subject matter expert in to the project can be the contingency plan.

Risk Transfer: Transferring the risk to someone. For Example, sub contracting a project to some other organization

Risk Acceptance: When the risk mitigation cost is more than the impact created by risk we may accept the risk. For example, usage of particular free tool increases effort in project, but the other commercially available are costlier and it would outweigh the current cost incurred by the increased effort, then we will just accept the risk.

Risk Management actions:

Every identified risk is detailed with source and category, they are evaluated for probability and impact, Risk exposure index is calculated and priority is updated. Then based on treatment strategy, risk mitigation action and contingency actions are entered appropriately. The actions are allocated to a person; the target date for completion of the action is entered.

Risks and their actions are evaluated on frequent basis (weekly/bi weekly) and the effectiveness of actions and trend of the risks are monitored.

Wherever the risk exposure index is not reducing, new actions are identified and tracked.

Risk log:

A simple mean to identify and track risks in one place in project,

Risk Detail	Source & Category	Probability	Impact	Risk exposure Index	Priority	Mitigation & Contingency action	Target date & Responsible	Status

Issue Management:

Any disruption, which is impacting the project adversely, is an issue. Risks when they realized in a project, it becomes issue. We may see a risk becoming issue or unexpected disruption coming in to project. In Issue management, the severities of Issues are logged and time priority is tracked. As already the issue is disrupting your project, there is no waiting period, a stringent set of timelines set to take corrective actions, however if the actions are not completed then its escalated immediately.

Issue Id	Date Raised	Issue Details	Severity	Time Priority	Corrective action	Target date & Responsible	Status

8 TAILORING AND WAIVERING

Organizational level defined processes may not be suitable to all projects as it is, and hence we have the concept called tailoring. Tailoring is more of pre-analyzed and pre-approved in nature. This is because at organizational level there will be tailoring guideline created and available on when tailoring can be performed, the different segments of projects and allowed tailoring for them are documented in that.

Organizations mostly classify their projects based on Size of the projects, technology and type of projects, and for each segments given here the allowable tailoring in terms of each process (activities tailoring and template tailoring) is pre identified/guidance given.

So projects can select the tailoring based on tailoring guideline, by considering the characteristics of project and client given requirements on process. Projects can list the entire processes and what activities are tailored and what not, along with template details. Normally this tailoring needs the Software Quality Analyst approval, who is assigned for the project.

Process Name	Tailored/ Waivered	Standard Activity	Tailoring & details	Standard Template	Tailoring & Details	Waiver & Reason
	Yes/No		Yes/No - <info>		Yes/No - <info>	

Waivering comes in to place when tailoring goes beyond the guideline and it's actually changes the process so much or a process itself is not followed. The waiver needs SEPG approval and delivery team approval, as not following a process or completely different process has its own impact and it has to be evaluated.

9 SOFTWARE ENGINEERING - DEVELOPMENT

Software development consists of Requirements, Design, Coding and Testing, build and release and Review activities. An understanding on these engineering activities helps the Software quality analyst to perform the job more effectively. We will see them in brief in this section,

Requirements Engineering:

Software Quality is greatly influenced with the quality of Requirements engineering process. The effort spent and validations performed in this phase always correlated with quality of outcome. In the initial days this phase was not really given that much importance and requirements engineering was not structured, hence the industry faced lot of problems. Over a period of time, when people understand that poor requirements capturing lead to most of the major failures, the requirements engineering concepts get strengthened and better structured activities are introduced in requirements engineering. As per IEEE the definition for Requirement is, " A condition of capability needed by a user to solve a problem or achieve an objective; A condition or capability that must be met or possessed by a system to satisfy a contract, standard, specification, or other formally imposed document"

Requirements engineering consists of requirements development and requirements management. In Requirements development, we have requirements elicitation, requirements description, requirements validation.

Requirements Elicitation:

There are various methods by which requirements can be collected from client. Not always we expect the client to give all requirements explicitly and many times they may assume few things, but as a development organization/service provider we can't be living with less information and provide a product which is not fit for use. If a patient comes to a doctor and tells his compliant to consult with the doctor, it's expected the doctor asks relevant questions and understands the condition well, before getting into solution, because the solution should be useful and cure the problem for the patient. In a similar way, it's the responsibility of software organization to enquire and collect the relevant information to build the software/provide service.

There are various techniques like observing the work, Apprenticing, interviewing the client, performing workshop, conference room piloting (in Packages this is normal technique) and throw away prototype.

Requirements Description:

The Requirements shall be documented in a formal manner. Most of the time Business Requirements are captured and then Software Requirements Specification document is created. The requirements are normally classified as Functional and Non- Functional requirements. Functional requirements are specific to the product features and Non functional requirements helps in ensuring the compliance, security, performance and other requirements which are needed for efficiency of software.

Use cases, Use case diagram, data flow diagram, Entity relationship diagram and other are common way of expressing the functionalities. Each requirement shall be uniquely traceable.

Software Requirements Specifications shall have the following details,

1.0 Software Application Scope
2.0 Overall Description
      2.1 Application Perspective
      2.2 User Characteristics
      2.3 Product Functions
      2.4 Assumptions and dependencies
      2.5 Requirements Subset

3.0 Functional Requirements

      3.1 Requirement <unique id>

            3.1.1   Inputs

            3.1.2   Process

            3.1.3   Output

            3.1.4   Testability

            3.1.5   Dependencies

            3.1.6   Data

            3.1.7   Reports (if any)

        <Repeat Requirements>

4.0 Specific Requirements

      4.1 Interface Requirements

      4.2 Report formats

5.0 Requirements Model

      5.1 Use case Diagrams

      5.2 Class Diagrams

      5.3 Data flow Diagrams

      5.4 Entity relationship Diagrams

6.0 Non Functional Requirements

      6.1 Performance

      6.2 Security

      6.3 Regulatory compliance

      6.4 Licensing requirements

      6.5 Safety

      6.6 Others

Requirements are analyzed for their applicability, achievability, completeness, etc and based on that they are moved to a particular module or to a particular release.

Requirements Validation: The Requirements captured are validated based on various available methods. Usage of prototypes, conference room piloting, performing meeting with client or review by client all of them contributing to validation of requirements. Requirements are reviewed internally before it's sent to client. Every organization supposes to have a review checklist to help the reviewer. However having a checklist with too many points is never a good way, as most of the time the checklist will be ignored in practical life.

Requirements Management:

Requirements are often tend to change or we found that few requirements can't be delivered in the way we planned. Hence management of requirements is key for successful delivery, in addition whenever there is change in scope, organizations face problem in finding the actual impact and in estimation. A well managed requirements list with adequate traceability helps in reducing this problem. Every requirement listed or identified shall be understood well by the design team, development team, testing team and by client. This understanding and clarifications makes things clear for the project team to work on. A bi-directional traceability matrix, with which we can trace a requirement from, business requirements ID ->software requirements ID->High level design section->Low level design section->program ID->unit test case ID-> Integration test case ID->System test case ID->Build ID-> Release ID, till release and from a release back to business requirement specification ID is possible with bi-directional traceability.

Bus. Req ID	Soft. Req ID	High Level Design	Low Level Design	Program ID	Unit test ID	Integration Test ID	System Test ID	Build ID	Release ID

Design Engineering:

Design Process helps in translating the requirements in to solution specifications. Design includes logical splitting of modules for better control and understanding. Structured design making with adequate guidelines and standards is the need of the hour for better designing. Designing involves three levels a) Architecture creation b) High level design creation and c) Low Level design creation.

Software Architecture defines the components of and relationships among all the software involved in developing, testing and operating the application. Architecture includes operating systems, databases, middle ware, different tiers involved, modules and applications involved. Architecture can consist of functional and physical depicture in nature. On need basis the architecture can be of detailed nature for each tier/database/network, etc separately defined.

Architecture shall be verified for scalability, maintenance, portability, performance, robustness and open standards. On developing the architecture there could be multiple options on selection of components or designing the layers itself, in such cases the alternates has to be captured and final decision to be derived based on formally evaluated benefits.

1. Introduction

    1.1 Scope

    1.2 Definitions/Acronyms/Abbreviations

    1.3 Conventions / Notations

    1.4 References

2. Architecture Objectives

3. Architecture Constraints

4. Alternatives considered

5. Alternative chosen with justification

6. Software Architecture

7. Hardware Architecture

8. Network Architecture

9. Functional Architecture

10. Database Architecture

11. External Interfaces

    11.1 Third party components

    11.2 Other applications

    11.3 Hardware Devices

12. Assumptions

High Level design

High level design presents the logical view of the physical computer implementation. The designer decomposes the system into software modules/components and identifies functionalities of each component keeping functional independence in mind. It specifies functional design, database design, communication design, user interface design, etc.

1. Overview

    1.1.   Introduction

    1.2.   Purpose

    1.3.   Scope

    1.4.   Definitions and Abbreviations

    1.5.   List of References

2. System Model

    2.1.   Implementation view of ERD/DFD

    2.2.   Use-Case Realizations

3. Logical View

4. Modules Interaction View

    4.1.   Modules Specifications

    4.2.   Module Integration details

5. Interface Details

    5.1.   User Interfaces

    5.2.   Software Interfaces

    5.3.   Hardware Interfaces

6. Security View

7. Deployment View

8. Implement View

    8.1.   Layers Overview

    8.2.   Components

    8.3.   Interface

9. Database View

Low level Design

Low level design provides detailed aspects which helps the developer to understand and code quickly. Some organizations may not have split of High Level and Low design, but instead one single design document. Getting too much detail in low level design is again based on criticality and cost/time involved in it.

1. Introduction

    1.1   Scope

    1.2   Definitions/Acronyms/Abbreviations

    1.3   Conventions / Notations

    1.4   References

2. Description of Units

    2.1 Unit Specifications

        2.1.1   Unit Specification ID

        2.1.2   Creation Date

        2.1.3   Screen Design

        2.1.4   Validation Logic

2.2   Units Integration Details

3.   Pseudo code

4.   Re-usable components

   4.1   Reusable components used

   4.2   Re-usable components to be developed

5.   Data Manipulations

6.   Error Processing

7.   Interfaces

8.   Performance

9.   Assumptions

It's important to ensure less coupling (high dependency between modules) and more of cohesiveness (internal elements binding in a module) is there in the design.

Coding and Testing:

Coding activity is the base where the product is realized in to an executable shape. Coding needs preparation, where the design and requirements are understood by the developers. They understand the development, test and production environments, so that deployment can be understood. Sometimes coding is based on component test cases developed over the low level design, this is test driven development. The developer may check for the exiting reusable code or open source code to use, however they have to be clear on the origin and understanding on the Intellectual property rights (what can be used and when, is it allowed, etc). They have to follow the coding standards and naming conventions when they code. The code may be daily integrated or weekly integrated or so on, hence the configuration practices identified for the team has to be followed. Enabling default editors in the coding environment helps to reduce the rework and improves code quality. Sometimes organizations think that defect is injected in this activity and that can be removed using adequate testing, this is a wrong conception. The defects are injected from requirements activity itself and the defect injected at that stage is more devastating than the defects injected at coding (though volume may be more)

Testing involves operating an application or application components under controlled condition to evaluate the results in order to discover the error. In Some cases, testing is used as qualifying the software. For better understanding on Testing definitions, please refer ISTQB (International Software Testing Qualification Board's materials and Knowledge areas) site.

There are different kinds of testing available and few of them are given for reference,

Black box Testing: Testing is based on functionality and the design and code is not validated in this.

Whit box Testing: Tests are based on coverage of code statements, branches, paths and conditions.

Smoke/sanity Testing: Initial testing to check if the software is good enough to take for detailed test.

Regression Testing: Re-testing after fixing of defects or modifications. Normally automated tests are used to reduce the human effort, in such cases, regression test scripts are written.

Load Testing: Testing the application under heavy loads to check when the application fails

Performance Testing: Under different condition how the performance/response of the application is tested

Security Testing: How well the system is protected from unauthorized access, intentional damages, etc. Penetration testing is performed to check possible penetration in to the system to check the various failure points.

Alpha Testing: Testing is performed in the organization itself with some other developers/ with potential users to check the product. This testing is performed before beta testing.

Beta Testing: Testing is performed by the end users in their environment and feedbacks are given, this is useful making minor changes before final release.

Acceptance Testing: Tests are performed by client or representative of client. The requirements agreed are tested in the client environment and this test helps to accept the software by client.

Levels of Testing:

Component/Unit Testing: This is the lowest level of testing and it concentrates on lowest unit verification. This testing is done by the programmer themselves with clearly written unit test cases. Sample of units are a screen, a message box, etc. In unit testing the basic fields, low level interfaces, unit boundaries are checked.

Integration Testing: Integration tests concentrates on verifying component interfaces, module interfaces. The target is to see if the integration works fine. Integration testing has many approaches like big band testing, bottom up testing, top down testing and sandwich testing.

System Testing: The test is performed to check is the software requirements are met with the final product. Testing is normally conducted on the complete system/application. The software is validated for functional and non- functional requirements. The system test environment should be a replica of client production environment as far as possible. Relevant clients supplied data can be used for this testing purpose.

Test Activities:

The testing process starts with understanding of the requirements and making a test strategy to test the product. Test Strategy can be documented as part of test plan or it can be a separate document. Test Strategy balances between cost of testing and Risk on product quality. A good testing will cover all the features and critical features adequately tested with, test cases with ability to discover defects. Checking the quality of testing is often difficult, however the process of testing can be controlled, test case coverage, verification of test cases can be performed. In some organizations they use prediction models, which are based defects identified in earlier phases using review and other techniques. When the predicted number of defects is not identified in testing, then the organization tries to understand or control the testing activities.

Test plan includes the following,

1.0 Introduction

1.1 Purpose

1.2 Scope

1.3 Acronym and Abbreviations

2.0 Test Strategy

2.1 Team Structure

2.2 Scope of Testing

2.3 Test Items

2.4 Features to be tested

2.5 Approach

3.0 Entry and Exit Criteria

3.1 Entry Criteria

<Describe the Entry Criteria for this Testing>

3.2 Exit Criteria

<Describe the Exit Criteria for this Testing>

3.3 Items Pass/Fail Criteria

3.4 Suspension and Resumption Criteria

3.5 Acceptance Criteria

4.0 Test Deliverables

5.0 Testing Tools

6.0 Testing Tasks

7.0 Test Configuration

7.1 Environment Needs

8.0 Responsibilities

9.0 Staffing and Training Needs

10.0 Schedules

11.0 Risks and Contingencies

12.0 Defect Reporting and Management

Test Case descriptions are normally part of a test log with unique id and traceability is established with the requirements. The tools which are used for managing the tests, has capability to enter the traceability with requirements, track the execution, log the defects and provide reports on defect age, trend, etc

Test Case ID	Description	Test Data	Expected Result	Pass/Fail Criteria	Tested By	Tested On	Priority	Fixed By	Fixed On	Verification Date

System test report issued by the testing department is mandatory for release, in some organizations. System report consists of final status of defects and how many are known, accepted and their criticality. It specifies the release version or builds which was tested and how many test cases are tested and coverage of testing, etc.

Build and Release:

The software is integrated as per the product integration plan and each

71

build is prepared with clear build note. Some of the newer technologies and tools are having continuous build, in such case the build details are maintained in the environment itself. Release process consists of verification of relevant items available for release (source code/programs/packages/user manual/installation manual/support documents/etc). Release checklist is often used to review the final set of deliverables and all relevant approvals from testing, quality assurance and design team should be available before release. In some organizations release audit is performed, this is important when its product development organization and when they do the launch.

Release Notes typically contains the following information,

- Product/Project details:

- Release Note version:

- Release Contents

Serial Id	Component Details	State of Release	Version

- System Requirement:

- Operating System Requirement:

- Dependencies:

- Known Issues:

- Mode of Delivery:

- Approvals:

10 SERVICE MANAGEMENT

Services are intangible in nature and can only be realized and also a service may reach the client immediately unlike a product. Hence service management has to be looked differently than product development. An organization should be prepared to deliver service with adequate preparation, before entering in to service delivery, as the services are immediately consumed by client.

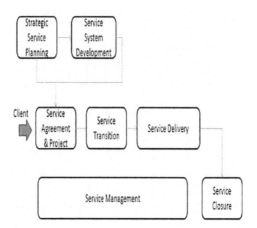

Organization prepares for Service delivery by analyzing their current capabilities and what kind of services they will be able to provide. The organization prepares the complete roadmap for a particular service, identifies the unique offerings, works on the cost and prepares a service catalogue. In this process they also evaluate the resources they have to provide such services. Where required they work on developing the service system (includes tools, methods, resources, reports, governance, etc). The identified services are offered to the client and based on the service catalogue and descriptions, the service agreement is established. Service agreements typically consists of different services, coverage, support durations, exclusion, service levels, penalty clauses, quality of service, etc.

The applications which have to be maintained or service details are transferred to the organization from client or from another vendor. Typically in service transitions the plans are made for application transfer, knowledge transfer, tool information transfer, process transfer and data transfer, etc. There are intermediate phases identified as required. The Service transition is evaluated using Transition Completion checks. Many organizations have predefined evaluation sheets and method to decide on service transition completion and they are reported to all the stakeholders and approval obtained.

Service delivery involves the agreed services being delivered as per the service agreement and maintaining of service system to deliver the services. This is a continuous process as per the agreed contract and normally of long duration. If the application maintenance is the service agreed then, incident management, service request management, problem management, change management and release management plays key role. In addition is the service desk has to be maintained by the organization, then they are established and service desk personnel are trained (normally in service transition itself).

Services are closed as per the agreed timeline, in case of no renewal of contract. In such a case the relevant documents are archived and knowledge transition to new service provider is given. In some cases the client might ask some support as technical expert, to be there with new vendor. Services are closed and financial accounts are closed and project given documents are stored in relevant repository. In case of a service phase out, the service line details are archived and relevant communications are made to the stakeholders.

Service Desk:

Service Desk is the first level interactive team with users and they capture and record the client given requests/complaints. Service desk can be central or distributed and they can be 24*7 or customized working days and hours based. Service desk people need customer facing skills and they are also provided with certain pre identified solutions and information details, which they themselves can share with users to close the request. Service desk team normally creates unique id for each requests/complaints, which can be traced for closure. The service entry system and transfer of tickets are typically automated with tools.

Service Request:

The service Requests are typically information request based and they can be with processing or without processing. The request and complaints are first analyzed and then it's determined whether it's a service request or incident (disruption to expected service for user), then service request is assigned to relevant team member who is available (as per plan). The service request is resolved and the status is updated for fix. The client confirmation and feedback is taken as needed.

Incident Management:

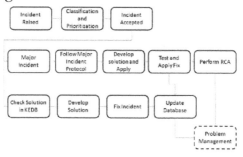

Incidents are raised by user and logged by service desk. The incidents are classified and prioritized like major incident, technical/application wise/etc, priority high, priority medium, priority low, etc. For major incidents there are typically criteria available to classify them and separate procedure available to inform relevant stakeholders and take immediate actions to restore the service back. Typically the major incidents are taken for further root cause analysis and it can initiate problem management. Whenever there is workaround identified and that can be used in similar conditions then knowledge database is updated. Typically high priority tickets may not have code fixes, and low priority tickets may have code fixes and then testing is performed and fix is applied afterwards. The users are informed on fix, and typically a time limit is given to user to respond for ensuring closure, else the status is moved to closure automatically.

Problem Management:

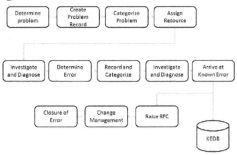

The repeated incidents, major incidents, trends (proactive problem management) are all triggers for problem management. Problem records are created and category is identified and resource is assigned. The problem is investigated and error record is created, further analyze on error, will help in understanding the error and solution related to it. This condition is known error and the Known error database is updated (KEDB). The relevant Request for Change (RFC) record is created and it goes through change management process to implement the solution.

Change Management:

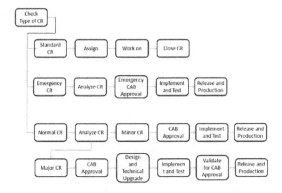

The Change request can be of standard change request, which is pre approved in nature, and changes are implemented and the change request is closed. In case of emergency change request the change approval board with emergency team with relevant protocol approves it and the changes are implemented and then changes are moved to production. In the context of normal change request, it's analyzed for minor and major CR and accordingly coding, testing, roll out plan and moving to production happens.

Release Management:

Release management plays vital role and release can be of full, delta or package release. Release management helps in ensuring the configuration management database and definitive software library and definitive hardware library are updated and relevant version of product/change is getting implemented. In addition roll out strategy and roll back strategy is made available. Release Manager Role is responsible for release to the production. Release plan includes training to relevant users also.

11 REVIEWS

Reviews are formal evaluation technique in which software requirements, design, or code are examined in detail by a group of persons other than the author(s) to detect faults, violations of development standards and other problems (as per IEEE Definition).

Typically reviews are used as part of Verification activities, however based on the context and purpose they can be validation method also. Reviews are considered as Static Verification and Validation method, whereas Testing is dynamic Verification and validation method. Reviews are typically used to detect defects at the early stage for removal. They reduce the overall rework cost compared to completely depending on testing activity to remove defects.

For Example, 1 requirement is addressed with multiple tables in design, with multiple programs in coding, many test cases are written in testing. If the requirement is wrongly written, reviews can eliminate the defect at the beginning in requirement phase itself, and can reduce unnecessary rework. Whereas if we wait for testing to find , that its wrong requirement , the rework increases also with too much expectation on testing activities, it may not deliver the expected results.

Activity	Req	Design	Coding	Testing	Client Acceptance	Hidden Defects

Defects Injection	10	15	100	5	0	NA
Reviews + Testing-Defect Removal	8	12	40	60	6	(130-126) = 4
Only Testing based Defect Removal	NA	NA	NA	90	20	(130-110)=20

In the previous table we can see, without adequate review, it's difficult for testing to detect all the defects and client will also find many defects in their acceptance testing.

Reviews are broadly of three types we can say, Technical reviews, Inspections, Walkthrough. We will see them briefly,

Technical Review:

The objective of technical reviews it to evaluate conformance to specifications and plans, also to ensure integrity. Technical reviews are performed with selected reviewers and they are qualified technically to review the work product. Reviews are performed on the documents like requirements specification, design document, test cases, etc. The document to be reviewed is sent even when 85% complete stage in some cases for ensuring, there is no separate cycle for rework. However in many cases the 100% complete document is sent for review. The review team may have leader when it group review, and he is responsible for preparation of final report. In case of Peer review, the identified peer will perform the review and will share the review comments. Reviews are formal in nature; however they are not too rigid. The review comments have to be addressed by the author of the document. In software industry we see many times this method being used, and especially in project/service organizations.

Inspection:

The objective of inspection is to detect defects in the work product and ensure that resolution is provided to that. Inspection is formal, structured with adequate supportive materials (checklist forms, etc). Inspections are planned well in advance in planning stages. The inspection team is identified, the moderator is identified, and every member in the inspection team is supplied with the work product/document. There is separate inspection meeting conducted, and the defects are discussed and moderator governs the meeting, a recorder records it. The rework has to be done by the author/producer based on the inspection report and they are followed up for closure. In product based organizations we can see inspection method usage.

Walkthrough:

The objective is to find defects, look for alternatives and this is also serves as learning forum. The producer/author walkthroughs document along with peers. The comments/observations are noted. The producer can decide on addressing the comments. The closure verification is performed in subsequent stages of development and not with any separate follow up. We can say this method is semi formal in nature. In software industry we see this method is used often in Code review, as code walkthrough. A walkthrough report is produced.

Sample review log,

Version No	Work Product Ref / Section ID	Review Comments	Severity	Defect Injected Phase	Type of Defect	Action Taken to Closure	Status	Remarks

Defects are logged with severity, defect injected phase and type of defect, these data in addition with defect causes will help in causal analysis, and prevention of defects in further projects and improve the process.

12 MEASUREMENT AND METRICS

Measurement is the process with which numbers are assigned to attributes of real world entities in the real world. We use the word measurement as process as well as describing attribute value also. Measurement is typically a direct quantification, which involves one single value, whereas Metric is an indirect quantification, which involves calculation and using more than one measure. Many a time, metrics gives us the relevant information, to take decision and to compare/benchmark performances. If we want to buy a car, and we want to know the efficiency of a car, we don't ask the measure of miles it can run or we don't ask how much gallon petrol can be filled in the car, we ask how much miles it can run for a gallon of petrol. This helps us to quantify as well as to compare with another car to understand the efficiency.

Similarly when it comes to software industry, if we want to know, out of 2 given projects which one is having better productivity, we need ask the effort as well as the size of product they produced. Without a metric (calculation based on measures) the comparison is not viable or useful. If you notice the two examples given here, we have spoken about efficiency when it comes to car and productivity when it comes to human. In fact calculation and measures involved wise they both are same (output/input), however for human we always measure (or use the word) productivity and for other non human resource we use the word efficiency.

Broadly software measures can be categorized as,

Process Metrics – used for quantifying process

Product Metrics – used for quantifying product and its quality

Project Metrics – used for quantifying project related performances

Resource Metrics- used for quantifying Resources usage/utilization, etc

Measurement activity involves cost, and having too many measures and useless measures will lead to inefficiency in the system and increased cost. As we know measures are important to understand the current status and to control the activities. If you are friend is waiting for you in a shop and he calls and asks you, how far you? Or how long it will take? You can't answer him that you are some distance away or long distance away, you need to quantify and tell him a value like 5 miles away or 20 minutes to reach. Basically numbers helps us to imagine and measures helps to build accuracy to imagination. Measures has to be accurate and precise, if we lack them, it will create bad reputation and adverse impact. We have to remember that data is costly.

So how do we identify which measures/metrics we need in our organization? For this it's better to use framework like Goal Question Metric to bring measures. In this method the Goal which we want to achieve is described and then relevant questions on what we want to know to achieve the goal is identified, then the metric which will give us the information and to control is identified. This is simpler and effective method to identify the metrics an organization needs.

Goal	To Reduce Defects in product	To Reduce Cost of product
Question	• What is current Defect Level • How much the testing is effective in removing defects	• Which phase contributes more effort • What is current productivity
Metric	Defect Density, Test Containment	Phase wise Effort Distribution,

	Effectiveness	Productivity

As discussed here, the metrics should be based on the organizational goal and need for information for decision making. However few metrics given here for your reference,

Metric	Type	Unit	Formula
Effort Variance	Project Metric	Percentage	(Actual Effort-Planned Effort)*100/Planned Effort
Schedule Variance	Project Metric	Percentage	(Actual End Date - Planned End Date)*100/ (Planned End Date - Actual Start Date)
Testing Defect Containment Effectiveness	Process Metric	ratio	Test Detected Defects/ (Pre and Post release defect)
Defect Density	Product Metric	Defect Count/Size Unit	Total Defects Detected/Size of product
Resource Utilization	Resource Metric	Percentage	Resource time logged *100/Total available time of resource in project
Productivity	Resource Metric	Size unit/Man days	Size of product/ Total Effort
Review Efficiency	Process Metric	Defect	Defects

		Count/Man hours	identified in Review/ Review Effort Spent

Service Management Metrics

Metric	Type	Unit	Formula
SLA Compliance	Project Metric	Percentage	(no. of total tickets closed within turnaround time)*100/No. of total tickets
Application Availability	Product Metric	Percentage	(Agreed Service Time-Down time during Agreed Service Time)*100/ (Agreed Service Time)
Change Request Closure ratio	Process Metric	Percentage	(Number of Change Requests Delivered*100/Nu mber of Change Requests Received)
Backlog Index	Project Metric	Percentage	(No of tickets in the month - No. of tickets closed in the month)*100/No. of total tickets in the month

The Metrics given here are called Lagging Indicators, as they can only explain the situation when the activity is completed, and they can only provide information that we need to control the future phase or period. There are few metrics which are called leading indicators, which can help us in prediction of future course. In a car when we read that how many miles we have crossed, it's more of lagging indicator, however if the car gives the predicted time to reach your destination with help of GPS (distance, traffic level, miles per hour), then these measures act as Leading Indicators. In software industry, Skill index, Requirements stability index, Size, design complexity and other measures which are either calculated at the beginning of project/phase or early phases of lifecycle, which with the help of a prediction model, if they are able to contribute to the prediction of final results, then they are leading indicators.

Metrics are too calculated in defined frequencies and it should be defined each metric. Typically weekly, monthly and milestone based frequencies are used. The calculation of metric and analysis should be done within few days from the last date which contributes to data, so that action implementation and its results can be studied in the next period.

Metrics are of no use unless they are analyzed and actions are taken. For analysis of metrics the right tools to be used. Graphical tools are of great help in analyzing the metrics. However right usage of tools is important and it shouldn't give wrong perspective of values. For showing percentage of different contributors/stratification in a metric, a pie chart is apt and usage of bar chart should be avoided. A bar chart is used more to show the count or discrete values of segments in a metric. So selection of charts has to be well understood and used. Similarly in a bar chart of value spanning to 1 to 100, if we show only 80 to 90 in an enlarged scale, the chart will look completely different.

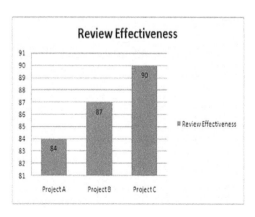

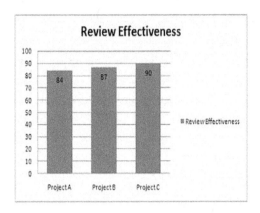

Now we can see how the charts can be manipulative, as the same values with different scales gives different perception. As long as you have smart audience and people who can spent time to understand, then you don't have problem otherwise you do have.

Important difference that people should know is the difference between efficiency and effectiveness. Effectiveness is always related to quality and it's a percentage measure and Efficiency is an energy measure and it could be of ratio or percentage.

Your organizational metrics program should take care,

- Don't just bring measures, just because they are popular in industry

- Don't measure individual as part of projects

- Appreciate data submission

- Convey importance of measure and educate on accuracy and precision

- Support with right tools

- Don't have high target, just because you have measures

- Ask for action items based on measure and convey the importance

- Try to collect measures as close to the actual work/activity/happening

13 CORE SQA ACTIVITIES

Software Quality Assurance activities are primarily performed by the member, who is identified as software quality analyst. This person provides project facilitation support, performs work product reviews, conducts quality gate review, Release checks and performs Audits. Though the responsibility of implementing the processes is there with project team, a Software Quality Analyst plays key role in ensuring that quality assurance activities are performed as expected.

Project Facilitation Support:

The Act in which an SQA supports a project by defining specific process elements, implementing them and ensures that the processes yields meaningful results to the project, is project facilitation. The SQA may need to perform various tasks to make the project aware of processes, train them, check the implementation, and do analysis so that the project is able to use the processes for successful delivery.

Project Kick off: Participate in project kick off and explain process planning and execution to team. Contract clauses are studied and understood by the SQA to ensure project delivers them.

Project Planning: Support the teams with relevant artifacts from quality management system; ensure that the team produces standard artifacts and where needed client instructions are followed. SQA is expected to have complete understanding of the quality management system and the options

available in it. Selection of lifecycles, selection of methods, relevant templates, etc has to be guided by the SQA. Similarly the organizational process assets like sample plans repository, estimation repository, risk repository, etc can be demonstrated by SQA to project to make them aware and use them. A SQA is expected to think as project manager and to support the project in building in a successful plan and SQA own the Quality assurance part of the plan. Quality assurance at project level doesn't stop with process and tools, an SQA may go and check if the verification and validation activities are appropriately planned, so that quality assurance of the product is a reality.

Estimation: SQA should be aware of the relevant estimation methods and he/she should be able validate the application of the methods, templates, tools and organizational metrics used (standard productivity), etc from the point of view of process. For example in estimation its expected the project team documents the risks and constraints and then add buffer or update any relevant variation to it, this step may not be followed by project team or project has added a buffer of 15%, whereas permissible limit it 5%, cases like this SQA should be able to point out and ask for approvals/technical review from senior delivery members.

Tailoring: Process planning is responsibility of project team and SQA. Considering SQA's have seen the process usage and process assets usage multiple times, they should be able to guide on selection of process and tailor them. How a tool expert guides the user on how to go about tool and what features are useful when, similarly SQA should be able to explain the process and what is appropriate when. Where required, SQA can help in customizing the process, templates, etc.

Training: SQA should be able to take training on the quality management system and its components as required. As many of the members in a project may need refresher or firsthand information on newer processes and templates, training at project level is effective in process implementation. In addition any specific training on causal analysis and metrics can be handled by SQA, where possible organizational level training can be conducted on these concepts.

Metrics Analysis support: The Metrics, its relevant template usage and interpretation of charts, understanding of data can be helped/supported by SQA. However preparation of metrics report and writing actions based on report shall be avoided by SQA. Considering an SQA understand the numbers and charts well, he/she can help a project team to understand them as well. However the numbers from project point of view can be only better visualized and owned by project team alone.

Causal Analysis: A SQA helps in performing causal analysis activity at project level. Whenever the final outcome is at risk due variation in intermediate phase outcome (ex: effort variance, defect rate, schedule variance, etc) the SQA based on the devised triggers can initiate the causal analysis along with the project manager. SQA can help project team with steps in causal analysis (usage of pareto to find significant category, usage of fishbone to find root cause, usage of brain storming to find solution, etc) and helps them to come out with action plans and support them in tracking to closure. The final changes in the actual outcome can be checked for improvement using hypothesis tests.

Ongoing support: SQA has to be kept engaged in project, so that the varying context in the project is understood by him, and the process planning is kept updated to suit that. In addition the timely intervention and support to project team is important to realize the product development with planned processes. For example, defects are normally captured for defect analysis which helps in defect prevention, but if for one week the activity is not happening due to certain constraints, the SQA should be available to monitor and raise this as a concern in the project meeting, so that the problem could be resolved quickly and corrective actions can be taken. However if the SQA is involved only in review, then he comes after a month and finds the problem, then no one will be ready to log the defects, as the volume they missed to log might be so high and project will try to avoid taking this job. Remember not all activities of quality assurance are directly contributes to realization of product in a project, some of them are linked to the organizational maturity and contribution to other projects. Hence people who think only for the project and for that instance may not be ready to support this. As a system what could improve in software industry is the indirect activities can be supported with tools for improving efficiency and people time spent is less in them. However be clear the tools also needs data in clear form, if Project enters defects or learning or risk in a messy form, the tool can't do much and Project effort will not go down. Sometimes people try to bring in lean concept to software practices, it's a welcome, however the discipline followed in all areas should also be considered, and not only the selected points of lean application. Similarly the less repetitiveness/uniqueness of projects is to be considered.

Work Product Reviews:

The SQA work product reviews are completely different from technical review. The purpose of this work product review is to ensure that the work product meets the quality standards, guidelines, templates, regulations and planned processes are used to produce the work product, along with completeness and integrity of the work product. The purpose is not to find defect, but the purpose here is to ensure compliance of work product with established standards.

Typically the following work products are reviewed by SQA,

- Project plan

- Estimation

- Support plans (Configuration plan, test plan, etc)

- Risk and Issue Management log

- Requirements Document

- Solution Design

- Code review reports

- Test cases

- Test execution report and defect closure

- Scheduling

- Metrics analysis reports

- Release plan

- Release artifacts

- Other agreed deliverables (as per contract and plan)

Release checks are basically performed before release and it's typically based on checklist. We have to remember our aim is to ensure quality product is delivered to client and with right configurations, the tools like process which we use is only to ensure we build quality product. So we should not be only bothered about process and even the results. Any poor result in one way means that we have to correct something in our process.

Quality Gates:

Quality Gates are normally identified points in lifecycle (end of phase/milestone) where the deliverables and status of project parameters are checked from quality assurance point of view. The concerns are highlighted and any critical deviation identified in quality gate reviews will ensure that it's resolved before moving to next phase. This is very important in product based organizations, as they can't afford to have products with defects sold to millions of customers. However many project/service based organizations also have adopted quality gates for better compliance and delivery.

Sample Quality Assurance plan template,

1. Introduction

1.1   Purpose and scope:

1.2   Project details:

2. SQA activities planned in Project:

2.1   Project Facilitation Activities:

2.2   Work Product Reviews:

2.3   Audits:

2.4   Reporting and Escalation:

3. Plan for Quantitative Management:

3.1 Quality Goals:

Objective	Target Value

3.2 Quantitative Baseline Reference:

4. Measurement and analysis plan:

4.1 Measurement objectives:

4.2 Metrics

1	Metric ID	
2	Metric Name	
3	Objective	
4	Measurements to be made	
5	Metric Description	
6	Source of Data	
7	Responsibility	
8	Frequency	
9	Reports Distribution	

4.3 Data Collection and Storage Procedures:

4.4 Analysis and Reporting Procedures

4.5 Methods and Tools

5. Quality Assurance and Defect Prevention:

5.1 Standards and Guidelines:

5.2 Tools:

5.3 Techniques and Methodologies:

5.4 Causal Analysis Details:

<Trigger, Analysis procedure, execution, proactive analysis, responsibilities>

6. Reference Documents:

<Test plan, Verification plan, project plan, etc>

14 QUALITY AUDITS

Audit - An objective examination of a work product or set of work products against specific criteria. Also audit is an evaluation of an organization, system, process, project or product against defined requirements. Audit is sampling based.

- "Systematic, independent and documented process for obtaining *audit evidence* and evaluating it objectively to determine the extent to which *audit criteria* are fulfilled."

- Audit evidence consists of "records, statements of fact or other information, relevant to the audit and which are verified."

- Audit criteria are a "set of policies, procedures, or other requirements against which collected audit evidence is compared."

Internal Auditing:

Internal Auditing is an independent, objective assurance and consulting activity designed to add value and improve an organization's operations.

It helps an organization accomplish its objectives by bringing a systematic, disciplined approach to evaluate and improve the effectiveness of risk management, control, and governance processes.

Audit Expectations:

An audit is expected to check, does the Quality System meet the requirements of the relevant Quality System Standard/model or Contract? Does the organization do what the Quality System specifies? Is the Quality System, as implemented, effective in ensuring maintenance and improvement of the quality of products and services?

Audit is not an alternative to an inspection operation and cannot serve as a crutch to an ineffective inspection or quality system

Types of Audit:

- First Party Audit (Internal Audits)

- Second Party Audit (Customer Audits)

- Third Party Audit (Audit Agencies)

Horizontal and Vertical Audits:

- Horizontal Audit - Assess same aspect in all projects.

- Vertical Audit - Assess all aspects in one project

    - forward tracking

    - backward tracking

- Hybrid Audits - Mixing Horizontal and Vertical Audits

Audit Team:

One or more auditors conducting an audit, supported if needed by Technical Experts. The auditors are lead by Lead Auditor. One or more auditees represent the function or the organization.

Lead Auditor Responsibilities: (Second party and Third party audits)

- Negotiate scope

- Selection of audit team

- Planning the audit

- Representing & Managing the audit team

- Opening & Closing Meeting

- Preparation & Submission of Report

- Quality Control of audit

Auditor Responsibilities:

- Communicating audit requirements to auditees

- Investigating through Interviews

- Documenting observations and evidence

- Verifying the effectiveness of Quality System

- Verifying the implementation of Processes in project

- Reporting results to the Lead Auditor/ Project team

- Assisting Lead Auditor (Second and Third party team)

Auditees Responsibilities:

- Being available for audit as per the schedule

- Co-operating with the auditor and providing factual information on the status of implementation of the quality system/Processes

- Agreeing on corrective actions / preventive actions and closing the non-conformances as per the target date

In Internal Quality Audits we may not have a lead auditor role mandatorily, that's the reason for mentioning second party and third party as reference on whenever we talk about lead auditor in this book.

Objective Evidences:

The objective evidences include documentations like plans, specs, code etc. Noting down the statement of what people told and observing auditees reaction and reviewing records.

In Internal Quality Audits, some organizations may only use documents and records as objective evidence.

Interviewing Expectations from Auditor:

- Listen attentively

- Don't disagree, criticize or interrupt

- Get agreement on your summary of what has been said

- Ask open ended questions

- Be polite and considerate for others feelings

Interview Questioning:

Open-ended questions

- do not presuppose the answer

- provide the opportunity for the interviewees to express their ideas and concerns

- allow for a spontaneous, unstructured response

Example: Please describe your role and responsibilities.

Direct questions

- may presuppose the answer (assumes something already exists)

- ask the interviewee for specific information

Example: Please tell us what criteria you use to perform your technical review evaluations.

Transition questions

- questions about questions

- used to guide the interview process

Example: Did we miss anything? Did you expect us to ask about anything else?

Closed end questions

- Providing the expected answer and understanding it happens are not?

Example: You are conducting monthly Reviews isn't it?

Terms to be clear in Audits:

Objective Evidence:

- Data supporting the existence or variance of something.

Non-Conformity:

- Non fulfillment of a requirement.

- Major nonconformity: The absence or total breakdown of a system to meet QMS requirements.

- Minor non-conformity: Systems are in place, but there is lack of evidence to support activities being done/lapse in implementation.

Correction:

- Action to eliminate a detected nonconformity.

Corrective action:

- Action to eliminate the cause of a detected nonconformity.

Preventive action:

- Action to eliminate the cause of a potential nonconformity.

Example: An observation, which specifies there is a potential non conformity. Like the technical specifications in a ERP projects is stored in windows file system, however considering the volume of such documents created in projects and versioning is only managed manually, the auditor can give observation, that project may have potential issue in later stage. Here the preventive action is applicable, as the non conformance is still not yet occurred. They can store the documents in a better configuration tool as part of preventive action.

Audit Process:

- Planning

- Audit Team Selection

- Audit Notification

- Opening Meeting

- Conduct of the Audit

- Closing Meeting

- Audit Report

When we do internal quality audit, we may not have opening meeting and closing meeting.

Planning an Audit:

The audit plan should be designed to be flexible in order to permit changes in emphasis based on information gathered during the audit, and to permit effective use of resources.

- Define the scope

- Refer the standard/model

- Estimate & define the schedule

- Identify the Auditees

- List the Auditors

- Get approval for plan

- Distribute to Stakeholders

Opening Meeting

- Brief the scope, announce the objective of audit and get commitment for audit from the stakeholders.

- Brief the audit code of conducts.

Conducting Audit

- The Audit should be conducted as planned by auditors and full support to be given by the auditees and Management. The audit checklist can be used for performing the audit by the auditor.

- Listen carefully for the expected and unexpected words

- Explore more on required context

- Use interview questioning methods

- Review documents based on defined process

- Have the checklist/model/standard

- Take notes appropriately

- Corroborate the documents and oral affirmation

Auditees can react in anyways like diversionary tactics, delaying tactics, Arguments about the 'practical significance', explaining the situation or providing expected answer.

Recording of evidence to take care; Deficiency or non-compliance must be a failure to comply with the letter or the intent of a requirement. Avoid placing blame on individuals by name. Mention the objective evidence in the non-compliance report

Preparation of Report:

Consolidate the reports and create summary based on findings. Create NC reports and observation.

It should be dated and signed by Lead Auditor in case of Second and Third party Audits

Audit report should contain the scope and objectives clearly and the details of audit (auditees, time, functions, etc) the reference standard/model/QMS system used should be listed. The Report should contain Nonconformities and Observations.

The Audit report should be distributed to all the relevant stakeholders.

Closure Meeting

- Present the report to senior management and auditees. Get the date of closure from the Auditees for identified NC's in their functions

Audit Follow up:

- The Auditees has to provide agreed timeframe to take correction, corrective action and preventive action (wherever applicable) based on audit report.

- The completion and effectiveness of corrective action should be verified.

- This verification may also be part of a subsequent audit.

15 QUALITY CONTROL TOOLS AND BASIC STATISTICS

The Quality Control tools are Seven and each of them has their own purpose and helps in better control.

a)   Check Sheet

b)   Flow Chart

c)   Pareto Chart

d)   Cause and Effect Diagram

e)   Histogram

f)   Scatter Plot

g)   Control Charts

Check Sheet:

They are used mainly categorize and count the data quickly on the field. We have to agree on how and what kind of data to collected, once the clarity is established, the data can be counted using this sheet.

For example, if we monitor the alert messages coming in 5 applications for half an hour to take count, we can mark one straight line for each count and once if we reach the fifth count it's marked by the crossed mark on the four lines. From 6th count to 9th line it's marked in the same way and 10th one is a crossed line. This helps in take count quickly under different category.

Applications	Alerts	Total Count
Application 1	𝄀𝄀𝄀𝄀 𝄀𝄀	7
Application 2	𝄀𝄀	2
Application 3	𝄀𝄀𝄀𝄀 𝄀𝄀𝄀𝄀 𝄀𝄀	12
Application 4	𝄀𝄀𝄀	3
Application 5	𝄀𝄀𝄀𝄀	4

Flow Chart:

These charts help us to distinguish the activities, and detail each activity in to multiple tasks, decision loops, data storage, etc. The chart also helps in identifying the problematic tasks or the activity which has less detail, and to concentrate in those activities to resolve it.

Pareto Chart:

Vilfredo Pareto the Italian economist used this chart in distinguishing the key factors which contributes significantly to the results. He used this chart demonstrate that 80% of wealth is there with 20% of population. This tool is highly used in performing causal analysis software industry in distinguishing which are the vital factors which we need to concentrate in analyzing any outcome.

To construct the chart we have to tabulate the data in descending order in a column and in another column we need to take the cumulative values. The causes or factors are listed in the horizontal axis. The frequency is given in the Y axis. We can draw vertical bars based on the factors and their frequency and use a line graph for the cumulative figure to draw. We can create a percentage scale on the right side vertical axis. A Pareto should have minimum 8 causes/factors in horizontal axis to draw; else it will not be useful.

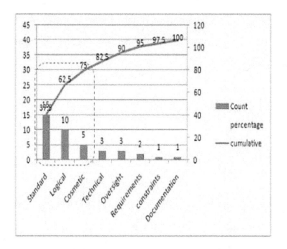

In the example given here on defects category and frequency of a testing in a project, we can see standard, logical and cosmetic defects are playing vital role in the total count. Hence we can concentrate on doing further analysis on these defects and try to reduce or prevent them.

Cause and Effect Diagram:

This diagram is also known as Fishbone diagram by it looks. This diagram is a way by which a problem/Effect can be looked in a structured way to identify causes under various influencing factors. The Effect is always entered in the right hand side and the bone is extended towards left. The factors which are influencing the effect are drawn as bones which are connected to the backbone drawn. Each of the major factors can be thought about and using different techniques like brainstorming and others, the causes which creates the effect is identified and they are connected in the relevant bone (factor). The different factors and the causes coming under that are identified and drawn. Wherever data exists that can be added to the causes to quantify that (even quick survey can help), so that we get clear idea, out of the few causes identified which one should be first resolved/corrective actions to be planned.

Histogram:

The purpose of histogram is to show the distribution of data. The study on central tendency and variation will help us to understand the behaviour of process.

Histogram can be manually also constructed, by using the formula (Highest value in data set –lowest value in data set)/ (total count of data points -1); we will get the width using this formula. The X axis to be plotted with 1 time width, 2 times width and so on. Now we need to plot the frequency of data in the region of width and construct this as bar graph.

Histogram helps us to quickly understand large amount of data coming from a process, by plotting. Histogram combined with Specification limit and calculation of capability helps in process capability analysis.

For example, we have 16 projects data on defect density, the histogram gives the graphical view which is easier for us to understand how the dispersion is.

Projects	Productivity
Project 1	0.78
Project 2	0.66
Project 3	0.71
Project 4	0.88

Project 5	1.1
Project 6	0.98
Project 7	0.55
Project 8	0.8
Project 9	0.94
Project 10	0.64
Project 11	0.72
Project 12	0.77
Project 13	0.84
Project 14	0.24
Project 15	0.45
Project 16	0.54

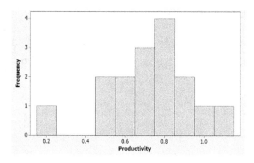

Scatter Plot:

This plot shows the possible relationship between two variables. This tool is useful when we want to understand the cause and effect relationship or to select variables to construct prediction models.

For example if we want to study productivity and customer satisfaction are they related, and then we can draw a scatter plot and study.

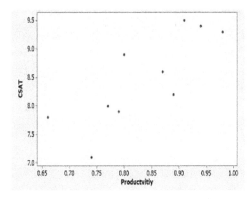

We can see weak positive correlation is there. It's weak because the points are not closer enough and it's positive since the X axis productivity increase the Y axis CSAT (Customer Satisfaction) increases. Like that we have a) weak negative correlation b) no correlation c) Strong positive correlation d) Strong negative correlation.

Remember the charts have no sense on their own; the logic has to be applied by human. If you put scatter plot data on rainfall in London and traffic jam in Mumbai, you may get strong correlation also, but it has no sense.

Control Charts:

Control charts are means of differentiating special cause of variation from common cause of variation. We take 3sigma as allowable variation, as economically its viable to control variation within that limits, and if we try to achieve 100% it will cost us more but returns will be less. Any data point beyond 3sigma we take as a special cause and we analyze. What it means if all the points are falling within the limits is that we are looking at a stable process. Control charts shall be used on data coming from a controllable process and not on something which is not controllable.

We can't use control chart to show rainfall in Paris, week by week, as that's not something which is controllable (better use some trend chart). Control charts shall be selected based on the type of data we have. However in software industry considering the uniqueness and tailoring, mostly I-MR (Individual Moving Range/ XMR) charts are used for all kind of data.

Total Process variation = Common Cause of Variation+ Special Cause of

Variation

Special Cause of Variation:

- Fluctuations not inherent to a process

- Data outside control limits or trend

- Represents problems to be corrected or improvements to incorporate into the process

Common Cause of Variation:

- Inherent random variations

- Consist of numerous small causes of random variability

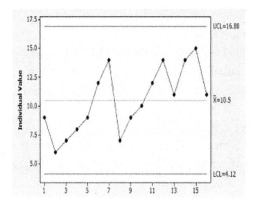

In the above given picture day wise review time spent is given. If by controlling review time, if the final value of interest Y (for example Defect containment effectiveness) can be achieved, then we might interested in controlling the review time. In this chart we don't see any point which is beyond the UCL and LCL whereas the UCL is mean+3 sigma and LCL is mean – 3 Sigma. UCL and LCL are control limits which are directly calculated from the data. These control limits are determined by inherent variation in the process. A data point beyond these limits indicates Special cause of variation and all the data points within the control limits are because of common cause of variation. In this chart there is no special cause of variation. Control limits are often called as Voice of Process. When there is very less data points the control limits derived will be only trail limits and as the data points increase (more than 27) the natural limits can be exhibited by the process. Whenever the special causes occurs they tend to change the control limits too much, in such case the special cause point has to be studies and corrective actions to be identified and worked on, in parallel the point can be removed from the plot and recalculation to be performed. Such removals should be recorded for the user reference.

Specification Limits are defined by the customer or by management, they are often called as Voice of Customer. They help to understand whether the process is capable enough to deliver the expectation.

Control charts helps mainly in statistical process control and the first step in establishing process control is to remove special cause of variation and ensure that process is stable. In order to check the process stability, we use the western electric rules (committee from western electric company presented this), which are set of rules applied to check the stability in control charts for the data from process.

- Any single data point falling above the $+3\sigma$ limit

- Two consecutive points falling above the $+2\sigma$ limit

- Three consecutive points falling above the $+1\sigma$ limit

- Seven consecutive points falling above the centerline

- Ten consecutive points falling below the centerline

- Six consecutive points falling below the -1σ limit

- Four consecutive points falling below the -2σ limit

In the example what we have given here, no test fails.

Process Capability:

- Process capability is the ability of a process to consistently meet specified customer-driven requirements

- Specification limits are set by management in response to customers' expectations

- The upper specification limit (USL) is the largest value that can be obtained and still conform to customers' expectations

- The lower specification limit (LSL) is the smallest value that is still conforming

A process is capable when the control limits are within the process specification limits. The process capability can be calculated using the relevant formula. Sometime people apply specification limits on the control charts, which can create confusion instead it can be applied on a histogram with the same data, which will be useful to interpret clearly.

Statistics Usage:
Some basic definitions to know:

Population: It is the group of all items of interest to a statistics practitioner.

Parameter: A descriptive measure of a population is called a parameter

Sample: It is a set of data drawn from the population

Statistic: A descriptive measure of a sample is called statistic.

In Statistics we have descriptive statistics (which gives details on characteristic of data) and Inferential Statistics (which is used to infer a set of data to make decisions).

Descriptive statistics provides a summary of characterization of a distribution (i.e. a set of numbers)

- A characterization of a central tendency (e.g. mean, median, and mode)

- A characterization of dispersion (e.g. variance, standard deviation, inter quartile range, and range)

Mean is the arithmetic average, Median is the central value of the given data set; Mode is the most frequently occurring data.

Central tendency implies location:

- Middle of group values

- Balance point

Dispersion implies spreads:

- Distance between values

- How much the values tend to differ from one another

These two are used together to understand to baseline of a process performance.

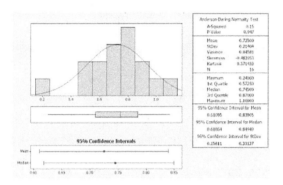

When the data is normal distribution we use mean as part of central tendency representation and we use standard deviation to imply dispersion. We can understand this by performing Normality Test. A tool like Minitab can give graphical distribution which also have Anderson-Darling Normality test results displayed (if P value greater than >0.05, then we consider as Normal Distribution).

Statistical Inference: The process of making an estimate, prediction, or decision about a population using sample.

Confidence level: is the proportion of times that an estimating procedure would be correct, if the sampling procedure is repeated for very large number of items. Mostly we use 95% Confidence level in software industry; however for stringent values 99% is also used.

In addition to this we need to know about different data types,

Discrete/Attribute Data:

Nominal: Categorical data where the order of the categories are arbitrary ex: development type, defect type

Ordinal: Nominal data with an ordering and may have unequal intervals. Ex: Priority levels, Severity

Continuous/Variable Data:

Interval: Continuous data that has equal interval. Ex: days, temperature

Ratio: Interval data set that has true zero value, and decimal values are possible. Ex: Defect Density, productivity, etc

Segmentation is related to Nominal data and Stratification is related to Ordinal data.

Hypothesis Tests:

A formal way of making a comparison and deciding whether or not the difference is significant, based on statistical analysis

Hypothesis testing consists of a null and alternative hypothesis:

- The null hypothesis states that the members of the comparison are equal; there is no difference (a concrete, default position)

- The alternative hypothesis states that there is difference; it is supported when the null hypothesis is rejected.

The conclusion either rejects or fails to reject the null hypothesis.

Remember the basis of this test is only based on null hypothesis and it's always the data are equal (sample belong to same population), and when a null hypothesis fails automatically we select alternate hypothesis.

P-value is the one based on which we can simply draw conclusion on the hypothesis test results. It's the probability value of the extreme values based on test statistic being part of the population, and when the probability value is below 0.05 (considering significance level of 5), then we reject null hypothesis as it's in the lowest probability region which is an error region (alpha). The simplest way we use this is, when P value is greater than 0.05

than we don't reject Null, when P value is lower than 0.05 than we reject Null Hypothesis.

Hypothesis test is mainly used in software to infer if the sample values we have drawn are representing the population, like productivity of 15 projects can be taken for hypothesis test to check do they represent the Organizational average 1.4 FP/effort. Similarly when a process is changed for improvement the results can be tested using hypothesis test to prove that statistically the new results are significant enough to claim the improvement. For example, Code review rate is 100 lines/hour and after change in process and introduction of tools, when we plot in control chart, we identify many points are going beyond the control limits and we would like to see if there is improvement in process behavior, so we select two sample hypothesis test to test if there is significant change, and if the null hypothesis is rejected (P value is less than 0.05) then we can prove that process has changed.

Hypothesis test selection is based on type of data, Normal distribution (parametric) or Non Normal Distribution (non parametric) and the number of samples to compare

Data Type (Column) Sample (Row)	Interval/Ratio Mean	Interval/ Ratio Variance	Ordinal Median	Ordinal Variance	Nominal Similarity
One Sample	1 sample T Test	1 sample Chi Square Test	1 sample wilcoxon Signed Rank test	1 sample kolmogoro v smirnov test	Chi Square
Two Sample	2 sample T test/ Paired T test	F test/ Levene Test	Mann Whitney test	Sigel Tukey test	Fisher Exact test
Multiple Samples	Analysis of Variance (ANOVA)/Multivariate Analysis of variance (MANOVA)	Bartlett Test/ Levene test	Kruskal Wallis Test	A van der wesrden normal score test	Chi-Square Test

In the below given table, we want to see if the review process is improved after adding a new review tool and change in process, so we test the data before and New data coming from the process, using hypothesis test.

Data type: Ratio, Distribution: Normal Distribution (in normality tests the samples shows P value greater than 0.05) and we have two samples with us. Hence considering the mean (Normal Distribution/parametric test), we go for two sample T test. Since the data is from same process, and checked after a period of time from same project, we go for paired T test.

Review Time	New Review Time
9	7
6	4
7	4
8	7
9	9
12	11
14	12
7	6
9	4
10	7
12	9
14	5
11	6
14	8
15	6
11	10

Null Hypothesis: Both samples are equal

Alternate Hypothesis: They are not equal

Hypothesis Test Results:

```
Paired T for Review Time - New Review Time

                  N    Mean    StDev   SE Mean
Review Time      16  10.5000  2.8284   0.7071
New Review Time  16   7.1875  2.4824   0.6206
Difference       16   3.31250 2.77414  0.69353


95% CI for mean difference: (1.83427, 4.79073)
T-Test of mean difference = 0 (vs not = 0): T-Value =
4.78  P-Value = 0.000
```

The test results show that P value is 0.00 < 0.05 which means reject null hypothesis, so the sample are not equal and it means there is significant change in process.

Control Charts, histograms and hypothesis tests along with statistical models (regression, logistic regression, dummy variable regression, etc) are highly used in software industry now a day, hence it's recommended for readers to spend time in this topic in researching and improving knowledge in this area.

16 STANDARDS (ISO 9001, ISO 20000, ISO 27001) AND MODELS (CMMI AND PCMM)

Standards specify the requirements, whereas the models share the best practices to be followed.

ISO 9001: 2008

Is a Quality management system requirements standard. The standard specifies the requirements which the organizations' quality management system to meet to get certified. The standard was last revised in 2008 and it's in use. ISO9001 is not a product/service certification and it's only applicable for the quality management system. However from a customer point of view what it means is, on any product/service defects, the customer can approach the certified organization and that will be addressed in systematic manner. Also the organization which is certified is keep working to improve the product quality and system in a continual manner.

The standard doesn't specify how exactly your processes should be or practices should be, but it gives the expectation on what it should meet.

ISO 9001 Standard Clauses:

Clause 1: Scope

Scope of application specifies on Quality management system and customer satisfaction expectations and applicable statutory and regulatory requirements

Clause 2: Normative Reference

Normative Reference which refers ISO 9000:2005

Clause 3: Terms and Definitions

Definitions and Terminologies, again this refers to all ISO 9000:2005 for referring them.

Clause 4: Quality Management System

- Quality Management System should be with mandated and required processes and their interaction and sequences well documented. Management commitment, resource availability and monitoring and measuring of the system along with continual improvement should be documented.

- Documentation requirements which specified Quality policy, quality manual should be available.

- Quality manual with scope of QMS, Exclusion and inclusion with standard's clause and scope of system to be mentioned along with process details.

- Document and Records controls expectations are given

Clause 5: Management Responsibility

- Management should show commitment in establishing policy, objectives, manual and communication on expectation on customer focus and implementation of the system

- Customer Satisfaction should be monitored and top management to be committed for this.

- Quality policy which is appropriate for the business and which communicates the intent of quality activities in the organization to be documented and maintained.

- Quality Objectives shall be established, which typically covers the projects and support functions performance objectives. There shall be a quality plan describing how they will be achieved and process will be formed and maintained.

- Organization should appoint a management representative who is from management and who will be responsible for QMS establishment, implementation and maintenance. He/she takes decision on behalf of management and promotes customer awareness.

- Responsibilities and Authorities to be clearly defined in the organization.

- Organization to have appropriate internal communication mechanism for communicating QMS effectiveness.

- Management Reviews shall be conducted at regular intervals (with Management Representative), which identifies changes needed in QMS, Policy and objectives, with consideration of Audit results, customer feedback, Non conformities in product, preventive and corrective action, follow up points from previous meeting, improvement proposals as inputs and could provide outputs like improvements implemented in QMS, product related improvements/changes, resource needs addressed, etc with all the activities and including the Management Review is recorded and maintained.

Clause 6.0 – Resource Management

- Adequate resources to implement the quality management system to be made available in the organization. Resources include human, software, hardware, facilities, safety, etc

- Human resources details on joining, induction, competency evaluation, training, deploying in work, responsibilities, evaluation to be maintained.

- Details of Infrastructure (hardware, software, facilities, etc) to be established with clear unique identification, ownership, assignment, tracking, transfer, close down; etc and periodical maintenance is expected.

Clause 7.0 – Product realization

- Product realization should have a plan (product plan/project plan) with details on objectives, process requirements, verification, validation, criteria for product acceptance, etc

- Customer Requirements to be collected, Review to be performed and Requirements should be agreed with customers

- Design and Development activities to be planned (Design, coding, review, testing) with adequate details.

- Develop design from Requirements, perform coding and develop relevant manuals to support the product.

- Perform periodical review of the project progress to ensure design and development commitment.

- Perform reviews and unit test on the intermediate work products (design document, code, etc) and check the final readiness

- Perform testing to validate the product using relevant testing (Integration testing, system testing, etc)

- Change Management should be followed on making any changes to product and its functionalities.

- To establish a purchase process and to have approved vendor list (based on periodical evaluation), maintain purchase order, invoices, delivery receipts, verification and acceptance records and adding to inventory.

- Establish traceability to product functionalities throughout development and control on process

- Track customer given documents/data separately and ensure the product and its components are kept with a configuration system.

- Any measuring and monitoring device used in projects should be calibrated.

Clause 8.0 – Measurement, Analysis and Improvement

- Measure customer satisfaction and take action as needed

- Have internal Quality Audit system established with clear objectivity, have annual/semi- annual quality plan, perform audits as per defined methods, record observations, distribute non conformances, follow up on verifying implementation of actions.

- Have measures to monitor the process performance, establish trends and take appropriate actions.

- Have measures to monitor the products, establish trends and take appropriate actions.

- Non conforming product (Defective) must be identified and controlled and appropriate resolution to be provided. The records shall be analyzed for corrective actions.

- Customer satisfaction, product quality, process performance, etc shall be analyzed and actions to be demonstrated.

- Continual Improvement plan should be available, which can be based on improvement request, corrective and preventive actions, client suggestions, Management Review Meeting guidance, etc

- Corrective and preventive actions identifications and application should be in a documented procedure and actions to be taken and improvement should be demonstrated.

To approach ISO 9001 Certification the QMS should be established and implemented for a period of more than 3 months (minimum), because 3 management review cycles and 2 Internal quality audits should be demonstrated to the auditors. A certification Agency (who is accredited to an Accreditation agency- who represents ISO in national/regional level) can perform third party Audit and issues certification. Pre-Audit can be used to validate few aspects of QMS with your auditors and Stage 1 audit is mainly focusing on scope, documentation of QMS and relevant records and Stage 2 concentrate on implementation and effectiveness of QMS. At the end of Stage 2 audit when there is no Major Non compliances and the minor non compliance are addressed than certification will be issued. Surveillance audit could be on annual/semi-annual basis, as requested by organization and end of 3 years re-certification is required.

ISO 20000-1:2011

This is a Service management system requirements standard. The standard specifies the requirements which the Service organizations' Service management system to meet to get certified. The standard was last revised in 2011 and it's in use. ISO20000-1 is not a Service Quality certification and it's only applicable for the Service management system. However from a customer point of view what it means is, on any service delivery problems, the customer can approach the certified organization and that will be addressed in systematic manner. Also the organization which is certified is keep working to improve the Service quality and Service system in a continual manner.

The standard doesn't specify how exactly your processes should be or practices should be, but it gives the expectation on what it should meet.

ISO 20000-1 Standard Clauses:

Clause 1: Scope

Scope specifies that this standard is can be applied by service seeking organization, Service provider and auditing bodies for conformity audits. The clause 4 requirements should be fulfilled by the service organization (which is seeking certification) on their own, and clauses 5 to 9 can be fulfilled with own activities or with the subcontracted/other parties who is performing them with agreement.

Clause 2: Normative Reference

There is no normative reference for this standard. However this clause is kept, to ensure uniformity in contents with other standards.

Clause 3: Terms and Definitions

Definitions and Terminologies are given in this section.

Clause 4: Service Management System General Requirements

- Top management shall demonstrate commitment to establish policy, objective, service management system, service planning, etc. Communicate the importance of Service Quality and Service Management system implementation. To conduct management reviews, ensure continual improvement and managing the risks to the services.

- Service Management Policy is established in the organization and its communicated and understood by all the employees

- The system should have clear roles, responsibilities and authorizes allocated to support the implementation

- Management Representative to be identified and he/she should be part of management team. The person is responsible for establishing service system, implementation and maintenance of the service system. The person is responsible for ensuring relevant resources are available, the system is operated, statutory and regulatory requirements are met and also to keep the management informed about it.

- Processes shall be established to ensure the supplier or internal groups are operating as per the expectations. The process interaction points, expectations, responsibilities and reporting shall be clearly mentioned. Wherever supplier is involved, supplier management process could be used to monitor and control and wherever internal groups are involved Service level management process can be used.

- Documents and records should be created to define, operate and control the Service management system, this includes, Service management policy, objectives, processes required, SLA's, service management plan, catalogue of services and other required procedures and records required by the standard.

- Documents should be created, reviewed, approved and changes are controlled, communicated and available for use, versioning and naming conventions to be followed, archive the obsolete documents and track the customer given/third party documents separately.

- Records should be legible, readily identifiable and retrievable. There shall be procedure for maintaining documents and records.

- Determine and provide resources like human, technical, and financial to ensure Service management system is established, operated and controlled. Human resources should tracked for their role, competency, training and evaluations and records to be maintained.

- Define Service management system scope, location, client, technology details. Create a service management plan to address, the objectives, system details, resources required, known limitations, policies, standards, statutory and regulatory requirements, authorities and responsibilities, involving supplier, integration of process and how effectiveness of service system will be monitored, controlled and improved. The plan shall be created, maintained and reviewed at regular intervals.

- The Service management system should be operated based on service management plan for design, transition, delivery and improvement of services. Service Management system should be operated by allocation of budget and funds, authority and responsibility allocation for resources, technical and financial resource allocation and monitoring, Identification and assessment of risk and handling them, Service process management and service management system operation.

- Service management system shall be monitored by internal audit program and by management review. The internal audit program shall be objectives and verify the ISO 20000-1 requirements, Service management system expectations and process implementation, the audit should have audit plan, execution as per plan and audit results communication. Follow up and closure of audit results is expected. The management review shall happen on periodical intervals, and to review the audit results, client feedback, Service non conformity, current and forecasted resource needs (human, technical, etc), risks, status of changes in Service management system, follow up actions from previous meeting, service improvement requests and others.

- Organization to have service improvement targets on quality, capability, cost, productivity, etc. To ensure the approved improvements are implemented, their effect on service improvements, improvements reporting. Revision of policies, procedures and roles to improve the service management system.

Clause 5.0: Design and Transition of new or changed services

- The Service provider shall take approval for new or changed services from client and interested parties to bring in. The change management process shall be applicable in changing the services. The planning for new or changed services to include, Authorities and responsibilities, activities, communication to interested parties, resource on human, technical, information and financial resource, time scale for planned activities, risk management, dependencies, testing, acceptance criteria for changed service, measurable service outcomes from new or changed services. The services which are removed have to be disposed appropriately with archival, disposal, etc. The service provider shall evaluate the ability of other parties involved and plan for meeting them.

- The new or changed service design and documentation shall include, authorities and responsibilities for new service, activities to be performed by customer, service provider and other parties, changed requirements for human resources, technical and information resources for new/changed services, changes to service management system, policies, new SLA's, new catalogues, procedures and measures to manage the new or changed services.

- The new or changed services shall be verified and tested for the plan and actual of the service requirements and design. The acceptance criteria and procedures shall be monitored for the changed services. The release and deployment process shall be used to deploy the services in the relevant areas.

Clause 6.0: Service Delivery Process

- The service provider should have an agreement on the services to be provided. The catalogue of services should have agreed SLA. The service provider can monitor and review the services as required and in planned intervals. The service provider should have an internal agreement with internal group and monitor and analyze them (for targets and components availability), to meet the service delivery. Results shall be monitored and as required causal analysis is performed to improve the delivery. Any changes to the service components shall be as per change management process.

- Service reports shall have clear identity, purpose, user details and service reports shall have details on performance targets and actual, major incidents/impacts, performance under heavy load, non conformities in service, trend information, customer complaints, satisfaction ,etc The actions shall be monitored and tracked to closure.

- Service provider should identify the different services and their expected level of service along with their service continuity. The requirements for service continuity and availability are determined based on agreement with client. Access right, end to end availability of service, service response times are identified for planning.

- Service continuity plan and availability plans to be prepared and maintained. Any change shall be as per change management process. Service continuity involves procedure on addressing a major loss/interruption, availability level targets, recovery phase and approach to be back to normal conditions. The service continuity plans, CMDB and other relevant data should be available to access at the time of major loss from other place.

- Service continuity and availability plans to be maintained. Availability levels to be monitored and reviewed and actions to be planned. Service continuity plans to be tested and availability plans to be tested and results to be recorded. Reviews should be conducted on the results and actions drawn.

- There shall be budgeting and costing for people, infrastructure, shared resources, overheads, capital and operating expenses, shared services, supplies, facilities, etc. The costing should include indirect costs also. The costing has to be approved by finance. The cost against the budget to monitored and budget revised accordingly or cost to be controlled.

- The Service provider shall maintain a capacity plan considering current capacity and forecasted requirements and expected capacity. Impact on availability, service continuity and service levels to be documented. The timescales, thresholds and cost for upgrading services to be detailed. Potential impact on new technology, statutory and regulatory requirements change shall be considered. The service provider shall monitor, analyze and tune service capacity.

- Information security policy is established, and risk assessment is performed and adequate controls are established. Information security audits are performed and improvements are identified. Any change Requests shall be assessed for information security risks, and updating the controls.

Clause 7.0: Relationship Process

- The service provider shall have a point of contact assigned to each client. The service reports to be shared with client and any feedback from the client shall be analyzed and appropriate action to be taken. There shall be documented procedure for client complaints handling, and accordingly every complaint to be recorded, analyzed and actions to be taken and reported back to client. Customer satisfactions shall be measured periodically and analyzed and actions to be taken.

- Service provider shall have supplier contract which includes, scope, dependency, service requirements, service levels, statutory and regulatory requirements to meet, capacity and availability requirements, contract exceptions, authorities and responsibilities, reporting mechanism, basis for charging, etc.

Clause 8.0: Resolution Process

- Incident management shall be there to record, prioritize, classify, Updation records, escalation, resolution, closure. Procedure for incident management and service request shall be established. Impact and priority to be documented, the team working on these incident and service request shall have access to known error, relevant details to access. The details of the status shall be documented for each incident. The release management process shall be used for releases. The customer shall be informed on the status, and whenever the service targets can't be met the customer to be informed. Documented definition of Major incident should be there and whenever major incident happens accordingly it should be handled. The top management shall be informed about the major incidents.

- Problem management shall be a documented procedure, and in problem management recording, prioritizing, classification, Updation of records, escalation, resolution and closure to be performed. The service provider shall analyze trend on incident and problem, and the root causes to be identified. Problems requiring changes to be raised with Request for change. Where root causes are identified and only temporary work around is there will result in known error. Effectiveness of known error and problem management should be monitored and analyzed and controlled.

Clause 9.0: Control Processes

- There shall be documented procedure for identifying and controlling of configurable item. Each of them should have unique identification, traceability with other CI, version, naming, etc and it should be part of CMDB and uniquely traceable. Baseline should be done for the CI's and the electronic and physical storage of CI's and back up to be monitored. Change management process shall be followed on changing the CI's. Configuration audits and status accounting should be performed on the CI's.

- Change management policy which determines CI's for change management, criteria used for determining changes which could give major impact should be established. Emergency changes shall have a procedure. Request for changes shall be impact analyzed, approved and development changes shall be performed. The changes to be tested before release. Schedule of changes shall be prepared with approved changes and deployment status and they should be followed. The CMDB to be updated for the relevant changes in CI. There shall be a back out plan established and maintained for roll outs.

- Service provider shall plan the release of changed services or components in discussion with the client and other parties. There should an emergency release definition and when to follow details. Releases to be tested prior to deployment. The acceptance test criteria shall be met and releases should be done in the live environment. The release success or failure shall be monitored and analyzed.

ISO 27001:2005

This is an Information Security Management System Requirements standard. This is adopted in most part of the world for Information Security controlling in IT organizations. There are 8 clauses in this standard.

Clause 1: Scope specifies the application of this standard to Information processing organizations and details it.

Clause 2: Normative Reference to ISO 17799:2005

Clause 3: Terms and Definitions are given

Clause 4: Information Security Management System Requirements

- Information Security Management System should be with mandated and required processes and their interaction and sequences well documented. Management commitment, resource availability and monitoring and measuring of the system along with continual improvement should be documented.

- Risk Assessment method and application and identification security threats and control using the control objectives shall be documented and maintained.

- Documentation requirements which specified Information Security policy, ISMS manual should be available.

- ISMS manual with scope of ISMS, Exclusion and inclusion with standard's clause and scope of system to be mentioned along with process details.

- Document and Records controls expectations are given in this standard.

Clause 5.0: Management Responsibility

- Management should show commitment in establishing Security policy, Security objectives, manual and communication on expectation on customer focus, security expectations and implementation of the system

- Information Security policy which is appropriate for the business and which communicates the intent of ISMS activities in the organization to be documented and maintained.

- Security Objectives shall be established, which typically covers the projects and support functions, infrastructure, Human resources, management, etc. There shall be a quality plan describing how they will be achieved and process will be formed and maintained.

- Organization should appoint an Information Security officer who is from management and who will be responsible for ISMS establishment, implementation and maintenance. He/she takes decision on behalf of management and promotes Security awareness.

- The Risks are assessed from business perspectives and relevant controls are applied after evaluation. Independent evaluation of Risk assessment is required.

- Statement of Applicability shall be prepared based on the threats and controls implemented for them and to be maintained.

- Responsibilities and Authorities to be clearly defined in the organization.

- Organization to have appropriate internal communication mechanism for communicating ISMS effectiveness.

Clause 6.0: Internal ISMS Audits

- Have internal Information Security Management System Audit system established with clear objectivity, have annual/semi- annual quality plan, perform audits as per defined methods, record observations, distribute non conformances, follow up on verifying implementation of actions.

- Information Security Audits shall verify the Risk Assessment method, Statement of applicability, control objectives implemented and the operational level security checks. Where required technical personnel support can be taken.

Clause 7.0: Management Review

- Management Security Reviews shall be conducted at regular intervals (with Information Security officer), which identifies changes needed in ISMS, Policy and objectives, with consideration of Audit results, customer feedback, threats to Information Security, Security incidents and events, preventive and corrective action, follow up points from previous meeting, improvement proposals as inputs and could provide outputs like improvements implemented in ISMS, Control related improvements/changes, resource needs addressed, etc with all the activities and including the Management Security Review is recorded and maintained. Infrastructure and resources to be reviewed for appropriateness and for security.

Clause 8.0: ISMS Improvement

- Measure Information Security effectiveness and take action as needed and measure the control objectives effectiveness and establish trends and take appropriate actions. Security Incidents and events must be identified and controlled and appropriate resolution to be provided. The records shall be analyzed for corrective actions.

- Risk Assessment method shall be revised as necessary and it should be as frequently whenever there is any change in any component in the system. The Statement of applicability should be revised as required.

- Continual Improvement plan should be available, which can be based on improvement request, corrective and preventive actions, client suggestions, Management Security Review Meeting guidance, etc. Corrective and preventive actions identifications and application should be in a documented procedure and actions to be taken and improvement should be demonstrated.

There are controls defined under 11 domains, 39 control objectives and 133 controls defined. The domains are,

- Security Policy
- Organization of Information Security
- Assets Management
- Human Resource Security

- Physical and Environmental Security
- Communications and Operations Management
- Access Control
- Information system acquisition, development and maintenance
- Information Security Incident Management
- Business Continuity Planning
- Compliance

The Risk assessment should take care the business process, assets involved, threats applicable, vulnerability to the threats, type of threat (confidentiality/integrity/Availability), threat level and vulnerability level, risk exposure level (based on business impact, risk level), Risk measure, applicable risk treatments and controls required. Risk assessment results should be repeatable and reproducible, hence defined methodology/tools are required to perform it.

Based on this Statement of Applicability is generated and relevant controls are implemented. The controls effectiveness is measured. The Risk Assessment is repeated on periodical intervals, as well as when there are new threats or business process changes happen.

CMMI (Capability Maturity Model Integration)

CMMI (Capability Maturity Model Integration) is a Process Improvement Model, which has collection of Industry best practices to implement in Organizations to achieve process capability and maturity. CMMI is a proven approach to achieve better performance results. CMMI is more of a framework which contains the model, trainings and appraisal components which helps an organization to implement the model in successful way to get benefit out of it. CMMI over the years has shown lot of success considering organizations are getting dramatic improvements in effectiveness, efficiency and quality.

The current version of CMMI is Version 1.3 and it got released in year 2010 and related appraisal version SCAMPI v1.3 also available. The model can be downloaded for free in CMMI Institute site. CMMI has three different Constellations in its product suite. As definition "a constellation is subset of

CMMI product suite relevant to improvement in a particular area of interest". The constellations are CMMI for Development, CMMI for Services and CMMI for Acquisition.

CMMI for Development - Addresses guidance on product/System development/Engineering

CMMI for Services - Addresses guidance on delivering services to internal and external entities

CMMI for Acquisition – Addresses supply chain management, acquisition and outsourcing processes in government and in Industry.

These CMMI Constellations are having set of Process Areas designed to achieve results in that area. However there are 16 common process areas between all the three models. The other process areas are specific to that constellation. In this book, we are limiting ourselves with CMMI Dev (CMMI for Development) and CMMI SVC (CMMI for Services). In CMMI Dev we have 6 specific Process Areas and in CMMI SVC we have 7+1 Specific Process Areas. The CMMI Dev consists in total 22 Process Areas and CMMI Svc consists in total 23(+ Service System Development) Process Areas.

Process Area is a cluster of related practices to achieve certain results. Process Areas are organized in terms of Goals and each Goal consists of set of practices, which would help to achieve the goals. An Example: Configuration related practices to be performed in product development or in Service Delivery are collected and established under one process area called "Configuration Management". Risk identification and handling practices are established under "Risk Management" process area.

CMMI consists of two representations, Staged Representation and Continuous Representation. Staged Representation is adopted by most of the organizations as its giving them guidance and benchmarking with other Organizations, Whereas continuous representation is adopted by Organizations which are clear in their area of improvement and are comfortable with the practices in all other areas (or comfortable with the level of performance).In Staged Representation, Organization's Maturity level is provided with 5 different process maturities. In Continuous

Representation, Each process Areas' capability levels are presented with 6 levels. A representation in CMMI is analogous to a view into a dataset provided by a database. Both representations provide ways of implementing process improvement to achieve business goals. Both representations provide the same technical content, but organized into different ways.

Maturity Level	Definition	Characteristic
Level 1	Initial	Poor Control & Heroism
Level 2	Managed	Project Processes & Reactive
Level 3	Defined	Organization Process & Proactive
Level 4	Quantitatively Managed	Predictable and controlled Process
Level 5	Optimizing	Process Improvement & Innovation

*source – CMMI Model

Maturity Level	CMMI Dev Process Areas	CMMI Svc Process Areas
Level 2	Requirements Management	Requirements Management
	Project Planning	Work Planning
	Project Monitoring and Control	Work Monitoring and Control
	Supplier Agreement Management	Supplier Agreement Management
	Configuration Management	Configuration Management
	Measurement and Analysis	Measurement and Analysis
	Product and Process Quality Assurance	Product and Process Quality Assurance
	------------	Service Delivery
Level 3	Requirements Development	Strategic Service Management
	Technical Solution	Incident Resolution and Prevention
	Product Integration	Service Transition

	Verification	Service Continuity
	Validation	Capacity and Availability Management
	Integrated Project Management	Integrated Work Management
	Risk Management	Risk Management
	Decision Analysis and resolution	Decision Analysis and resolution
	Organizational Training	Organizational Training
	Organizational Process Definition	Organizational Process Definition
	Organizational Process Focus	Organizational Process Focus
	-----------	Service System Development*(Add)
Level 4	Quantitative Project Management	Quantitative Work Management
	Organizational Process Performance	Organizational Process Performance
Level 5	Organizational Performance Management	Organizational Performance Management
	Causal Analysis and Resolution	Causal Analysis and Resolution

*Add – Additional Process Area: Applicability decided by Need of the Organization

CMMI Development – Sample artifacts details for reference.

Process Area- Specific Goals & Specific Practices	Typical CMMI Artifact
Requirements Management	
SG 1 Manage Requirements	
SP 1.1 Understand Requirements	Requirements Document\ Collection of requirements & mails

SP1.2Obtain Commitment to Requirements	Sign off on Requirement\agreement on requirements
SP 1.3 Manage Requirements Changes	Change log
SP 1.4 Maintain Bidirectional Traceability of Requirements	Traceability matrix
SP 1.5 Ensure Alignment between Project Work and Requirements	Updation of project plan
Requirements Development	
SG 1 Develop Customer Requirements	
SP 1.1 Elicit Needs	Requirements meeting MOM/prototype
SP 1.2 Transform Stakeholder needs into Customer Requirements	Business Requirements
SG 2 Develop Product Requirements	
SP 2.1 Establish Product and Product-Component Requirements	Software Requirements Specification document
SP 2.2 Allocate Product-Component Requirements	Software Requirements Specification document
SP 2.3 Identify Interface Requirements	Interface Requirements in SRS
SG 3 Analyze and Validate Requirements	
SP 3.1 Establish Operational Concepts and Scenarios	Use Case ,timeline scenarios, etc
SP 3.2 Establish a Definition of Required Functionality and Quality Attributes	activity diagram, use case
SP 3.3 Analyze Requirements	Requirements defect/review
SP 3.4 Analyze Requirements to Achieve Balance	Requirements allocation/module wise requirements, risks
SP 3.5 Validate Requirements	Analysis with client/prototype etc
Technical Solution	

SG 1 Select Product-Component Solutions	
SP 1.1 Develop Alternative Solutions and Selection Criteria	Alternative solutions/evaluation report/selection criteria
SP 1.2 Select Product-Component Solutions	Documented solution
SG 2 Develop the Design	
SP 2.1 Design the Product or Product Component	Product Architecture
SP 2.2 Establish a Technical Data Package	Technical data package
SP 2.3 Design Interfaces Using Criteria	Interface design/Criteria/Low Level design
SP 2.4 Perform Make or Buy Analysis	make/buy/reuse analysis
SG 3 Implement the Product Design	
SP 3.1 Implement the Design	Source code
SP 3.2 Develop Product Support Documentation	user manual/product manual
Product Integration	
SG 1 Prepare for Product Integration	
SP 1.1 Establish and Integration Strategy	Integration Strategy
SP 1.2 Establish the Product Integration Environment	Product integration strategy to have environment details
SP 1.3 Establish Product Integration Procedures and Criteria	Product integration plan
SG 2 Ensure Interface Compatibility	
SP 2.1 Review Interface Descriptions for Completeness	Integration review checklist
SP 2.2 Manage Interfaces	updated interfaces/MOM
SG 3 Assemble Product Components and Deliver the Product	

SP 3.1 Confirm Readiness of Product Components for Integration	Build readiness check
SP 3.2 Assemble Product Components	Build
SP 3.3 Evaluate Assembled Product Components	Release Readiness Checklist
SP 3.4 Package and Deliver the Product or Product Component	Release Note/Release
Verification	
SG 1 Prepare for Verification	
SP 1.1 Select Work Products for Verification	Reviews/Unit test plan
SP 1.2 Establish the Verification Environment	Templates/checklists/tools, etc
SP 1.3 Establish Verification Procedures and Criteria	Reviews/Unit test plan(procedure)
SG 2 Perform Peer Reviews	
SP 2.1 Prepare for Peer Reviews	peer review schedule/meeting planning, etc
SP 2.2 Conduct Peer Reviews	peer review report
SP 2.3 Analyze Peer Review Data	Defect closure
SG 3 Verify Selected Work Products	
SP 3.1 Perform Verification	Unit testing
SP 3.2 Analyze Verification Results and Identify Corrective Action	Defect Analysis & Defect prevention
Validation	
SG 1 Prepare for Validation	
SP 1.1 Select Products for Validation	System Test plan
SP 1.2 Establish the Validation Environment	Test Environment set up

SP 1.3 Establish Validation Procedures and Criteria	System Test plan
SG 2 Validate Product or Product Components	
SP 2.1 Perform Validation	Test Execution Results
SP 2.2 Analyze Validation Results	Defect Analysis & Defect prevention
Project Planning	
SG 1 Establish Estimates	
SP 1.1 Estimate the Scope of the Project	Top Level WBS, work Package description
SP 1.2 Establish Estimates of Work Product and Task Attributes	Size, estimating model
SP 1.3 Define Project Life Cycle	Life cycle documented (mostly in Project plan)
SP 1.4 Determine Estimates of Effort and Cost	Effort & cost of project (mostly in Project plan)
SG 2 Develop a Project Plan	
SP 2.1 Establish the Budget and Schedule	Budget and schedule (mostly Kick off/initiation deck etc)
SP 2.2 Identify Project Risks	Risk Identification checklist/Risk log
SP 2.3 Plan for Data Management	Data Management plan (mostly in project plan/charter)
SP 2.4 Plan for Project Resources	Project resources (mostly in project plan/charter)
SP 2.5 Plan for Needed Knowledge and Skills	Skill Matrix by roles
SP 2.6 Plan Stakeholder Involvement	Stakeholder Matrix
SP 2.7 Establish the Project Plan	Project plan
SG 3 Obtain Commitment to the Plan	

SP 3.1 Review Plans that Affect the Project	Revised plan/Review comments
SP 3.2 Reconcile Work and Resource Levels	Revised Plan
SP 3.3 Obtain Plan Commitment	Approval & Plan commitment from stakeholders
Project Monitoring and Control	
SG 1 Monitor Project Against Plan	
SP 1.1 Monitor Project Planning Parameters	Effort, schedule, other measures (Metrics report)
SP 1.2 Monitor Commitments	Commitment monitoring (Meeting MOM/issues, etc)
SP 1.3 Monitor Project Risks	Risk Log/weekly/biweekly/monthly reports
SP 1.4 Monitor Data Management	Data Confidentiality/availability and integrity monitoring (Meeting MOM)
SP 1.5 Monitor Stakeholder Involvement	Stakeholder participation (Meeting MOM)
SP 1.6 Conduct Progress Reviews	Monthly reviews/biweekly reviews
SP 1.7 Conduct Milestone Reviews	Milestone meeting (Sometimes Monthly/biweekly reviews)
SG 2 Manage Corrective Action to Closure	
SP 2.1 Analyze Issues	Issue Log
SP 2.2 Take Corrective Action	Action items (mostly in MOM or in a log/tool)
SP 2.3 Manage Corrective Action	Action Closure status and details (mostly in MOM or in a log/tool)
Risk Management	
SG 1 Prepare for Risk Management	
SP 1.1 Determine Risk Sources and Categories	Risk Source and category (can be part of Risk log/sheet and applied to each risk)
SP 1.2 Define Risk Parameters	Risk Parameters typically impact *

	probability =>Risk Exposure
SP 1.3 Establish a Risk Management Strategy	Strategy document/guidance in Risk log itself (threshold/mitigation/contingency/acceptance/avoidance/roles)
SG 2 Identify and Analyze Risks	
SP 2.1 Identify Risks	List of Identified risks (risk log)
SP 2.2 Evaluate Risks	Risk Exposure and priority
SG 3 Mitigate Risks	
SP 3.1 Develop Risk Mitigation Plans	Mitigation actions (to reduce risk exposure-mostly in risk log)
SP 3.2 Implement Risk Mitigation Plans	Action closure and Risk rating modifications
Configuration Management	
SG 1 Establish Baselines	
SP 1.1 Identify Configuration Items	Configurable items list (mostly in Configuration plan)
SP 1.2 Establish a Configuration Management System	Configuration repository, approval mechanism (mostly in configuration Plan)
SP 1.3 Create or Release Baselines	Baselines list/criteria (mostly in configuration plan)
SG 2 Track and Control Changes	
SP 2.1 Track Change Requests	Change requests logged
SP 2.2 Control Configuration Items	Change requests status update
SG 3 Establish Integrity	
SP 3.1 Establish Configuration Management Records	Status Accounting /configuration history reports
SP 3.2 Perform Configuration Audits	Configuration audit(functional/physical)
Measurement and Analysis	

SG 1 Align Measurement and Analysis Activities	
SP 1.1 Establish Measurement Objectives	Define measurement objectives (org level can be mapped to project level)
SP 1.2 Specify Measures	Effort/defect/schedule/utilization, etc
SP 1.3 Specify Data Collection and Storage Proc	data source, collection, frequency(metric guideline/report itself)
SP 1.4 Specify Analysis Procedures	procedure to analyze (graphs/chart/points to consider)
SG 2 Provide Measurement Results	
SP 2.1 Obtain Measurement Data	Metrics Report
SP 2.2 Analyze Measurement Data	Metrics Report
SP 2.3 Store Data and Results	Metrics Report
SP 2.4 Communicate Results	Meeting minutes/monthly/bimonthly reports
Process and Product Quality Assurance	
SG 1 Objectively Evaluate Processes and Work Products	
SP 1.1 Objectively Evaluate Processes	Audit report (Process Audit)
SP 1.2 Objectively Evaluate Work Products and Services	Work product Review Report (SQA review on deliverables)
SG 2 Provide Objective Insight	
SP 2.1 Communicate and Ensure Resolution of NC Issues	Non compliance closure Report
SP 2.2 Establish Records	Non compliance closure Report
Integrated Project Management	
SG 1 Use the Project's Defined Process	Tailoring
SP 1.1 Establish the Project's Defined	tailoring checklist/document (of

Process	organization process with project context)
SP 1.2 Use Organizational Process Assets for Planning Project Activities	estimation/measurements/risks, etc used for planning (mostly in project plan)
SP 1.3 Establish Project's work Environment	Documented Project environment (mostly in project plan)
SP 1.4 Integrate Plans	integrated project plan
SP 1.5 Manage the Project Using the Integrated Plans	Revised integrated project plan/updates based on it
SP 1.6 Establish Teams	Team roles and guidance (Mostly in project plan)
SP 1.7 Contribute to the Organizational Process Assets	Lessons learnt/best practices/improvements, etc
SG 2 Coordinate and Collaborate with Relevant Stakeholders	
SP 2.1 Manage Stakeholder Involvement	Team Meetings/issue log/Project meetings
SP 2.2 Manage Dependencies	Issue ,dependency log & closure of actions
SP 2.3 Resolve Coordination Issues	Issue ,dependency log & closure of actions
Organizational Training	
SG 1 Establish an Organizational Training Capability	
SP 1.1 Establish the Strategic Training Needs	Linked training needs with business objectives (mostly annual Training plan /strategy document)
SP 1.2 Determine Which Training Needs Are the Responsibility of the Organization	Project level & Org level training - listed (in plan)
SP 1.3 Establish an Organizational Training Tactical Plan	Training Calendar
SP 1.4 Establish Training Capability	Training environment, trainer details documented at org. level

SG 2 Provide Necessary Training	
SP 2.1 Deliver Training	Training delivery record (Invite/material/feedback/attendance)
SP 2.2 Establish Training Records	Training delivery record (Invite/material/feedback)
SP 2.3 Assess Training Effectiveness	Training feedback evaluation/360 feedback/performance check, etc
Organizational Process Focus	
SG 1 Determine Process-Improvement Opportunities	
SP 1.1 Establish Organizational Process Needs	Process Needs & details (mostly in Quality Manual)
SP 1.2 Appraise the Organization's Processes	Audit/appraise/review organization process
SP 1.3 Identify the Organization's Process Improvements	Improvement log (based on appraisals and from projects)
SG 2 Plan and Implement Process Actions	
SP 2.1 Establish Process Action Plans	Improvement Log (with CR/improvement and action plan)
SP 2.2 Implement Process Action Plans	Improvement Log status(with CR/improvement and action plan)
SG 3 Deploy Organizational Process Assets and Incorporate experiences	
SP 2.1 Deploy Organizational Process Assets	Deployment plan with status
SP 2.2 Deploy standard processes	Deployment plan with status
SP 2.3 Monitor the Implementation	Deployment plan with status
SP 2.4 Incorporate Experiences into the Organizational Process Assets	Updated Repositories (Estimation/risk/defects/samples, etc)

Organizational Process Definition	
SG 1 Establish Organizational Process Assets	Define Processes
SP 1.1 Establish Standard Processes	Documented process Definitions
SP 1.2 Establish Life-Cycle Model Descriptions	Lifecycle description (waterfall/incremental/iterative, etc)
SP 1.3 Establish Tailoring Criteria and Guidelines	Tailoring Guideline (mostly by process) and Criteria (small/large, etc)
SP 1.4 Establish the Organization's Measurement Repository	Metrics repository
SP 1.5 Establish the Organization's Process Asset Library	Repositories (Estimation/risk/defects/samples, etc)
SP 1.6 Establish work Environment Standards	Work Environment details (mostly in Quality manual)
SP 1.7 Establish rules and guidelines for teams	Teaming norms (mostly in Quality manual)
Decision Analysis and Resolution	
SG 1 Evaluate Alternatives	
SP 1.1 Establish Guidelines for Decision Analysis	Guideline (when to use, criteria, responsible, etc)
SP 1.2 Establish Evaluation Criteria	Criteria to evaluate decision(it will vary based on the context)
SP 1.3 Identify Alternative Solutions	Document alternate solution (separate DAR sheet used in many org.)
SP 1.4 Select Evaluation Methods	Evaluation techniques (Pugh matrix, cost benefit, weighted average, etc) (DAR sheet to have the method)
SP 1.5 Evaluate Alternatives	Valuation of each alternative solution (DAR sheet)
SP 1.6 Select Solutions	Final Solution (DAR sheet)

145

CMMI Services – Sample Artifact for reference

Process Area- Specific Goals & Specific Practices	Typical CMMI Artifact
Configuration Management	
SG 1 Establish Baselines	
SP 1.1 Identify Configuration Items	Configurable items list (mostly in Configuration plan)
SP 1.2 Establish a Configuration Management System	Configuration repository, approval mechanism (mostly in configuration Plan)
SP 1.3 Create or Release Baselines	Baselines list/criteria (mostly in configuration plan)
SG 2 Track and Control Changes	
SP 2.1 Track Change Requests	Change requests logged
SP 2.2 Control Configuration Items	Change requests status update
SG 3 Establish Integrity	
SP 3.1 Establish Configuration Management Records	Status Accounting /configuration history reports
SP 3.2 Perform Configuration Audits	Configuration audit(functional/physical)
Measurement and Analysis	
SG 1 Align Measurement and Analysis Activities	
SP 1.1 Establish Measurement Objectives	Define measurement objectives (org level can be mapped to project level)
SP 1.2 Specify Measures	Effort/defect/schedule/utilization, etc
SP 1.3 Specify Data Collection and Storage Procedures	data source, collection, frequency(metric guideline/report itself)
SP 1.4 Specify Analysis Procedures	procedure to analyze (graphs/chart/points

	to consider)
SG 2 Provide Measurement Results	
SP 2.1 Obtain Measurement Data	Metrics Report
SP 2.2 Analyze Measurement Data	Metrics Report with Analysis
SP 2.3 Store Data and Results	Metrics Report in Database & Communication
SP 2.4 Communicate Results	Meeting minutes/monthly/bimonthly reports
Process and Product Quality Assurance	
SG 1 Objectively Evaluate Processes and Work Products	
SP 1.1 Objectively Evaluate Processes	Audit report (Process Audit) with Noncompliance & corrective actions Audit checklist
SP 1.2 Objectively Evaluate Work Products	Process QA Review Report
SG 2 Provide Objective Insight	
SP 2.1 Communicate and Resolve Noncompliance Issues	Non compliance closure Report Mail of report being shared with stakeholders
SP 2.2 Establish Records	Audit plan Non compliance closure Report Status of corrective actions
Requirements Management	
SG 1 Manage Requirements	
SP 1.1 Understand Requirements	Requirements Document\ Collection of requirements & mails
SP 1.2 Obtain Commitment to Requirements	Sign off on Requirement\agreement on requirements
SP 1.3 Manage Requirements Changes	Change log

SP 1.4 Maintain Bidirectional Traceability of Requirements	Service Requirements traceability matrix Requirements tracking system
SP 1.5 Ensure Alignment between Work Products and Requirements	Updation of project plan
Supplier Agreement Management	
SG 1 Establish Supplier Agreements	
SP 1.1 Determine Acquisition Type	Type of Suppliers and Acquisition types
SP 1.2 Select Suppliers	Supplier list and Vendor Evaluation sheet
SP 1.3 Establish Supplier Agreements	Purchase Order, Contract, SOW
SG 2 Satisfy Supplier Agreements	
SP 2.1 Execute the Supplier Agreement	Receive Product, Track Supply - Tracking status
SP 2.2 Accept the Acquired Product	Acceptance report, inception report
SP 2.3 Ensure Transition of Products	Transition plans, handover report Training reports
Service Delivery	
SG 1 Establish Service Agreements	
SP 1.1 Analyze Existing Agreements and Service Data	Analysis of past SLA's and SOW & Analysis of reports
SP 1.2 Establish the Service Agreement	Service agreement/ Contract etc
SG 2 Prepare for Service Delivery	
SP 2.1 Establish the Service Delivery Approach	Project/Service management plan with the agreed Service delivery approach (Incident/problem, etc)
SP 2.2 Prepare for Service System Operations	Validation of Knowledge Transfer/ Validation of Service System tool (training etc)/ operational readiness assessment
SP 2.3 Establish a Request Management	Incident Management tool/ Log

System	
SG 3 Deliver Services	
SP 3.1 Receive and Process Service Requests	Incident Management record in the tool/ Log
SP 3.2 Operate the Service System	Service logs from the tool/ Performance Status reports
SP 3.3 Maintain the Service System	Corrective or preventive maintenance change requests/ Change Requests on the service system
Work Planning	
SG 1 Establish Estimates	
SP 1.1 Establish the Service Strategy	Service Strategy Document
SP 1.2 Estimate the Scope of the Work	Top Level WBS, work Package description
SP 1.3 Establish Estimates of Work Product and Task Attributes	Size, estimating model
SP 1.4 Define Lifecycle Phases	Life cycle documented (mostly in Project /Service management plan)
SP 1.5 Estimate Effort and Cost	Effort & cost of project (mostly in Project plan)
SG 2 Develop a Work Plan	
SP 2.1 Establish the Budget and Schedule	Budget and schedule (mostly Kick off/initiation deck etc)
SP 2.2 Identify Risks	Risk Identification checklist/Risk log
SP 2.3 Plan Data Management	Data Management plan (mostly in project plan/charter)
SP 2.4 Plan the Resources	Project resources (mostly in project plan/charter)
SP 2.5 Plan Needed Knowledge and Skills	Skill Matrix by roles
SP 2.6 Plan Stakeholder Involvement	Stakeholder Matrix

SP 2.7 Establish the Work Plan	Project plan/Service Management Plan
SG 3 Obtain Commitment to the Plan	
SP 3.1 Review Plans That Affect the Work	Revised plan/Review comments
SP 3.2 Reconcile Work and Resource Levels	Revised Plan
SP 3.3 Obtain Plan Commitment	Approval & Plan commitment from stakeholders
Work Monitoring and Control	
SG 1 Monitor the Work Against the Plan	
SP 1.1 Monitor Work Planning Parameters	Effort, schedule, other measures (Metrics report)
SP 1.2 Monitor Commitments	Commitment monitoring (Meeting MOM/issues, etc)
SP 1.3 Monitor Risks	Risk Log/weekly/biweekly/monthly reports
SP 1.4 Monitor Data Management	Data Confidentiality/availability and integrity monitoring (Meeting MOM)
SP 1.5 Monitor Stakeholder Involvement	Stakeholder participation (Meeting MOM)
SP 1.6 Conduct Progress Reviews	Monthly reviews/biweekly reviews
SP 1.7 Conduct Milestone Reviews	Milestone meeting (Sometimes Monthly/biweekly reviews)
SG 2 Manage Corrective Action to Closure	
SP 2.1 Analyze Issues	Issue Log
SP 2.2 Take Corrective Action	Action items (mostly in MOM or in a log/tool)
SP 2.3 Manage Corrective Actions	Action Closure status and details (mostly in MOM or in a log/tool)
Capacity and Availability Management	
SG 1 Prepare for Capacity and Availability Management	

SP 1.1 Establish a Capacity and Availability Management Strategy	Service management plan with details on Human/Infra/technological capacity and availability for agreed service
SP 1.2 Select Measures and Analytic Techniques	Capacity and availability measures and analysis technique
SP 1.3 Establish Service System Representations	process simulation (system simulation), Simulation of inflow and capacity and availability with excel
SG 2 Monitor and Analyze Capacity and Availability	
SP 2.1 Monitor and Analyze Capacity	Trend charts on service resource usage data
SP 2.2 Monitor and Analyze Availability	Trends on availability, analysis and action
SP 2.3 Report Capacity and Availability Management Data	Service system performance reports Service availability reports
Decision Analysis and Resolution	
SG 1 Evaluate Alternatives	
SP 1.1 Establish Guidelines for Decision Analysis	Guideline (when to use, criteria, responsible, etc)
SP 1.2 Establish Evaluation Criteria	Criteria to evaluate decision(it will vary based on the context)
SP 1.3 Identify Alternative Solutions	Document alternate solution (separate DAR sheet used in many org.)
SP 1.4 Select Evaluation Methods	Evaluation techniques (Pugh matrix, cost benefit, weighted average, etc) (DAR sheet to have the method)
SP 1.5 Evaluate Alternative Solutions	Valuation of each alternative solution (DAR sheet)
SP 1.6 Select Solutions	Final Solution (DAR sheet)
Incident Resolution and Prevention	
SG 1 Prepare for Incident Resolution and	

Prevention	
SP 1.1 Establish an Approach to Incident Resolution and Prevention	SQP with details on Service Incident handling approach
SP 1.2 Establish an Incident Management System	Service Incident logging Tool/ Log
SG 2 Identify, Control, and Address Individual Incidents	
SP 2.1 Identify and Record Incidents	Service Incident ticket record
SP 2.2 Analyze Individual Incident Data	Major incident, repeat incident analysis
SP 2.3 Resolve Incidents	Updated resolution in the tool/ log
SP 2.4 Monitor the Status of Incidents to Closure	Closure Service incident log/ Status update/ Escalation data (mail/tool ref etc)
SP 2.5 Communicate the Status of Incidents	Status reports/ Communication mail
SG 3 Analyze and Address Causes and Impacts of Selected Incidents	
SP 3.1 Analyze Selected Incidents	Report of underlying causes of incidents/ Documented causal analysis activities
SP 3.2 Establish Solutions to Respond to Future Incidents	Knowledge data base
SP 3.3 Establish and Apply Solutions to Reduce Incident Occurrence	Change in Service Delivery system like a tool/ procedure / policies etc.
Service System Transition	
SG 1 Prepare for Service System Transition	
SP 1.1 Analyze Service System Transition Needs	Compatibility analysis of current and post-transition service systems Baseline service system components Mitigations for of identified transition Issues and risks
SP 1.2 Develop Service System Transition Plans	Transition plans for service system transition (tools, process, competency)

SP 1.3 Prepare Stakeholders for Changes	Strategy of training and transition Transition communication and notification artifacts (e.g., emails, system announcements, bulletin boards)
SG 2 Deploy the Service System	
SP 2.1 Deploy Service System Components	Installation records Installation instructions Operational scenarios and procedures
SP 2.2 Assess and Control the Impacts of the Transition	Post deployment review Back out / rollback results, if needed Service impacts due to deployment issues
Service System Development	
SG 1 Develop and Analyze Stakeholder Requirements	
SP 1.1 Develop Stakeholder Requirements	Customer requirements End-user requirements
SP 1.2 Develop Service System Requirements	Service system Requirements & software requirement specification
SP 1.3 Analyze and Validate Requirements	Prototype, Validation of requirements
SG 2 Develop Service Systems	
SP 2.1 Select Service System Solutions	Architecture of solution, Service system design
SP 2.2 Develop the Design	Code and develop service software, develop components of service system
SP 2.3 Ensure Interface Compatibility	Interface identification within components and external components of service system
SP 2.4 Implement the Service System Design	Implemented service system components Training materials User, operator, and maintenance manual
SP 2.5 Integrate Service System Components	Service system integration plan, build the service system

SG 3 Verify and Validate Service Systems	
SP 3.1 Prepare for Verification and Validation	Verification tools, environment, test strategy, simulation plan
SP 3.2 Perform Peer Reviews	peer review checklist, peer review report
SP 3.3 Verify Selected Service System Components	Review and unit test
SP 3.4 Validate the Service System	Validation reports and results, Test Results
Integrated Work Management	
SG 1 Use the Defined Process for the Work	
SP 1.1 Establish the Defined Process	tailoring checklist/document (of organization process with project context)
SP 1.2 Use Organizational Process Assets for Planning Work Activities	estimation/measurements/risks, etc used for planning (mostly in project plan)
SP 1.3 Establish the Work Environment	Documented Project environment (mostly in project plan)
SP 1.4 Integrate Plans	integrated project plan
SP 1.5 Manage the Work Using Integrated Plans	Revised integrated project plan/updates based on it
SP 1.6 Establish Teams	Team roles and guidance (Mostly in project plan)
SP 1.7 Contribute to Organizational Process Assets	Lessons learnt/best practices/improvements, etc
SG 2 Coordinate and Collaborate with Relevant Stakeholders	
SP 2.1 Manage Stakeholder Involvement	Team Meetings/issue log/Project meetings
SP 2.2 Manage Dependencies	Issue ,dependency log & closure of actions
SP 2.3 Resolve Coordination Issues	Issue ,dependency log & closure of actions

Strategic Service Management	
SSG 1 Establish Strategic Needs and Plans for Standard Services	
SP 1.1 Gather and Analyze Data	Analyzed data on the organization's capabilities (past performance report) Analyzed data on strategic needs, Analysis report
SP 1.2 Establish Plans for Standard Services	Strategic plan on standard service, catalogue, needs
SG 2 Establish Standard Services	
SP 2.1 Establish Properties of Standard Services and Service Levels	Critical attributes of standard services Organization's set of standard service levels Common and variable parts of standard services
SP 2.2 Establish Descriptions of Standard Services	Service Catalog with specific instructions
Service Continuity	
SG 1 Identify Essential Service Dependencies	
SP 1.1 Identify and Prioritize Essential Functions	Risk Assessment, Business continuity assessment report
SP 1.2 Identify and Prioritize Essential Resources	prioritization based on Assessment (Business continuity assessment report)
SG 2 Prepare for Service Continuity	
SP 2.1 Establish Service Continuity Plans	Business Continuity plan
SP 2.2 Establish Service Continuity Training	Service continuity training material Training records
SP 2.3 Provide and Evaluate Service Continuity Training	Training Records on business continuity
SG 3 Verify and Validate the Service	

Continuity Plan	
SP 3.1 Prepare for the Verification and Validation of the Service Continuity Plan	Plan for Business continuity check
SP 3.2 Verify and Validate the Service Continuity Plan	Review report
SP 3.3 Analyze Results of Verification and Validation of the Service Continuity Plan	Results of Simulation Test report & improvement recommendations
Risk Management	
SG 1 Prepare for Risk Management	
SP 1.1 Determine Risk Sources and Categories	Risk Source and category (can be part of Risk log/sheet and applied to each risk)
SP 1.2 Define Risk Parameters	Risk Parameters typically impact * probability =>Risk Exposure
SP 1.3 Establish a Risk Management Strategy	Strategy document/guidance in Risk log itself (threshold/mitigation/contingency/acceptance/avoidance/roles)
SG 2 Identify and Analyze Risks	
SP 2.1 Identify Risks	List of Identified risks (risk log)
SP 2.2 Evaluate, Categorize, and Prioritize Risks	Risk Exposure and priority
SG 3 Mitigate Risks	
SP 3.1 Develop Risk Mitigation Plans	Mitigation actions (to reduce risk exposure-mostly in risk log)
SP 3.2 Implement Risk Mitigation Plans	Action closure and Risk rating modifications
Organizational Training	
SG 1 Establish an Organizational Training Capability	

SP 1.1 Establish Strategic Training Needs	Linked training needs with business objectives (mostly annual Training plan /strategy document)
SP 1.2 Determine Which Training Needs Are the Responsibility of the Organization	Project level & Org level training - listed (in plan)
SP 1.3 Establish an Organizational Training Tactical Plan	Training Calendar
SP 1.4 Establish a Training Capability	Training environment, trainer details documented at org. level
SG 2 Provide Training	
SP 2.1 Deliver Training	Training delivery record (Invite/material/feedback/attendance)
SP 2.2 Establish Training Records	Training delivery record (Invite/material/feedback)
SP 2.3 Assess Training Effectiveness	Training feedback evaluation/360 feedback/performance check, etc
Organizational Process Focus	
SG 1 Determine Process Improvement Opportunities	
SP 1.1 Establish Organizational Process Needs	Process Needs & details (mostly in Quality Manual)
SP 1.2 Appraise the Organization's Processes	Audit/appraise/review organization process
SP 1.3 Identify the Organization's Process Improvements	Improvement log (based on appraisals and from projects)
SG 2 Plan and Implement Process Actions	
SP 2.1 Establish Process Action Plans	Improvement Log (with CR/improvement and action plan)
SP 2.2 Implement Process Action Plans	Improvement Log status(with CR/improvement and action plan)

SG 3 Deploy Organizational Process Assets and Incorporate Experiences	
SP 3.1 Deploy Organizational Process Assets	Deployment plan with status
SP 3.2 Deploy Standard Processes	Deployment plan with status
SP 3.3 Monitor the Implementation	Deployment plan with status
SP 3.4 Incorporate Experiences into Organizational Process Assets	Updated Repositories (Estimation/risk/defects/samples, etc)
Organizational Process Definition	
SG 1 Establish Organizational Process Assets	Define Processes
SP 1.1 Establish Standard Processes	Documented process Definitions
SP 1.2 Establish Life-Cycle Model Descriptions	Lifecycle description (waterfall/incremental/iterative, etc)
SP 1.3 Establish Tailoring Criteria and Guidelines	Tailoring Guideline (mostly by process) and Criteria (small/large, etc)
SP 1.4 Establish the Organization's Measurement Repository	Metrics repository
SP 1.5 Establish the Organization's Process Asset Library	Repositories (Estimation/risk/defects/samples, etc)
SP 1.6 Establish Work Environment Standards	Work Environment details (mostly in Quality manual)
SP 1.7 Establish Rules and Guidelines for Teams	Teaming norms (mostly in Quality manual)

PCMM (People Capability Maturity Model)

The People Capability Maturity Model (People CMM) is a *"framework"* that helps organizations to successfully address their critical people issues. Based on the best current practices in fields such as human resources, knowledge management, and organizational development, the People CMM guides organizations in improving their processes for managing and developing their workforces.

- Software Engineering Institute (SEI) is the producer of this model

- Organizations like IBM, Microsoft, Citibank, Boehm, etc., having contributed for bringing out the first version of P-CMM released in the year 1995.

- Releases:

1995- PCMM version 1.0

2001- PCMM version 2.0

The People CMM provides guidance to organizations in selecting immediate improvement actions that help organizations

- Characterize the maturity of their workforce practices

- Integrate workforce development with process improvement

- Become an employer of choice

- Improve the ability of organizations to attract, develop, motivate, organize and retain talent.

- Ensure alignment between the individual goals and organization's goal.

- Develop workforce required to execute business strategy.

- Prioritize activities for improving workforce capability

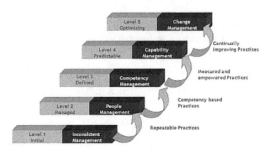

The model has five maturity level and the details of process area is given below,

Level	Focus	Process Areas
5 Optimizing	Capability & performance are continually improved	Continuous Workforce Innovation Organizational Performance Alignment Continuous Capability Improvement
4 Predictable	Capability is managed quantitatively and the organization exploits opportunities in its competency framework	Mentoring Organizational Capability Management Quantitative Performance Management Empowered Workgroups Competency-Based Assets Competency Integration
3 Defined	Organization develops a framework of workforce competencies required to accomplish its business objectives	Participatory Culture Workgroup Development Competency-Based Practices Career Development Competency Development Workforce Planning Competency Analysis
2 Managed	Managers take responsibility for managing and developing their people	Compensation Training and Development Performance Management Work Environment Communication and Coordination Staffing
1 Initial		

For detailed reference please visit: sei.cmu.edu and www.cmmiinstitute.com

17 AGILE SCRUM

There are many agile methodologies available like Scrum, Extreme Programming, Feature driven development, agile data, etc Out of these Scrum is popular and most used IT Project/service based organizations. The scrum principles are easy to understand, it can be used with different technologies and tools.

Scrum is a framework structured to support complex product development. Scrum consists of Scrum Teams and their associated roles, events, artifacts, and rules. Each component within the framework serves a specific purpose and is essential to Scrum's success and usage. (Scrum Guide, 2009)

Scrum Principles:

- Time box

- Cross functional teams

- Transparency

- Priority driven

- Demonstration of results

- Responsiveness to change

Scrum Process:

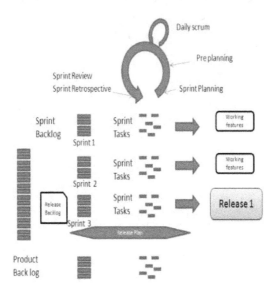

Scrum Team:

Scrum Team consists of Scrum Master, Product owner and Scrum Team (development team). The teams are self organizing and cross functional in nature and also expected to be smaller in size 6 to 9 people.

Scrum Master is a process coach, team facilitator and removes road blocks. He ensures that scrum theory; principles are adhered and limit the interaction with others (outside team) with team as needed.

Product Owner is responsible for product and its functionality. He adjusts priorities and feature list in product backlog. Product owner is one person. He accepts or rejects the results of work. He provides adequate information to development team for understanding the work.

Scrum Team/Development Team is with individuals who are responsible for the product. Cross s functional team consists of developer, tester and QA/Designer (as required); however they may not be called with those roles inside the project. The team should self organize themselves and ensure they understand the work and deliver working product.

Sprints in Scrum:

A Sprint is a time boxed effort to deliver working software. Normally it spans between 2 to 4 weeks. A sprint has work items in sprint back log prioritized, and any change within the sprint is not accepted, else the sprint will be restarted. A sprint has planning meeting, review and Retrospective meetings.

Release:

The identified feature for working software is derived from the product backlog and relevant numbers of sprints are identified. Usually a release is made in once in 3 months.

Backlogs:

The Scrum project has different backlogs created and maintained to facilitate results.

Product Backlog:

Based on product strategy, the project identifies the features required for the product and the product back log contains all the functionalities and features listed and reviewed. Releases can be identified with it and relevant sprints are identified. The product owner is responsible for maintaining the features.

Sprint Backlog:

This contains the features and functionalities expected in a sprint. Technical requirements, design can be part of the sprint back log. User stories are typically part of the backlog.

Sprint Activities:
Sprint Planning:

A preplanning happens in the previous sprint to understand the goals and at the beginning of a sprint the planning meeting happens to fix the objectives and functionalities. Product owner details the definition and features. From product backlog the relevant features are taken for the sprint. Based on the user stories the tasks are identified. Product owner, scrum master and the development team is involved.

Daily Scrum:

They do a stand up meeting for 15 minutes, and they check what has been done from previous meeting, what will be done before next meeting and what constraints they have. Based on that, the team works on their daily task.

Sprint Review:

The product demonstration is given to the product owner. The product owner can accept or reject the d product features.

Sprint Retrospective:

Sprint retrospective meeting is mainly for the team and they discuss, what went well, what can be changed, etc this helps in continually improving and organizing themselves

Sprint Tasks:

- Tasks are derived based on Sprint back log

- Estimate the tasks using any of Fibonacci, T shirt sizing or poker methods

- Interdependencies are considered

- Development team selects the work tasks

- Tasks are completed as per the priority

- Relevant outputs are stored (wiki page/design/test cases/ code in environment)

- The uncompleted tasks (features) are moved back to the product log

- Working features are demonstrated in the Sprint Review meeting

Definition of Done is the criteria based on which a user story will be considered as completed.

Burn down Chart is used to monitor the effort availability with the user stories to be developed.

Velocity is a measure used to determine the speed of completion. It is the story points completed (as per definition of done) in a sprint. A team's velocity is more useful measure, if we monitor that in at least few sprints. This measure helps in determining the timeline required for release.

18 EARNED VALUE ANALYSIS

Earned Value Analysis is technique that helps to understand the deviations in the project parameters early and correct them. The method gives estimated value at the time of completion, which helps us to understand, what will be the cost at the time of completion. In this method scope, schedule and cost are integrated together. This method is not a statistical prediction model, as it doesn't consider the inherent variations (range) and instead predicts a single point value.

With Earned Value Analysis, the risks are managed well, the projects are aware of deviations in schedule and cost variance, and effective control is possible, all tasks are included in calculation and less error.

As we know that, first we form the scope (detailed work break down structure) and then we schedule and allocate resources (cost). These three are together expressed in earned value method and cost unit is commonly used to measure and predict. After forming the schedule we allocate the effort by resource which results in cost. The month by month or milestone based cost is available with us based on our work break down structure, this forms the planned value. At any point in time in a month we know what is the planned value of cost for those tasks supposes to be completed on that point in time.

As a slight variation to traditional Earned value analysis, we can assume effort wherever the word cost comes in. This is because, in organizations they don't monitor in terms of cost. Others can follow it as cost. The Earned value is at any point in time, what is the % of work completed and what is the planned value in proportion of completion, they have earned. In a case where requirements activities are allocated with 1000$ (planned value) for 10 tasks, and by the date of expected completion when we check, they have only completed 70% of work (only 7 tasks), then the Earned Value is 700$. Assume to complete the 7 tasks itself, they have spent 900$ (actual value) instead of their earned value of 700$, then we can understand there is variation.

Schedule variation can be understood by looking at the 10 tasks completion on expected date is not done but only 7 are performed. Hence if you take (Earned Value- Planned Value) we can easily understand it's of -300$. Any value in Negative means we are delayed, and anything in positive means we are advance in schedule. Remember in Earned Value, we use single measure cost to represent other parameters. However it's proportionate and understandable. The same is calculated as Schedule performance Index (SPI) with (Earned Value/Planned Value). Here we have (700/1000), which is 0.7. Anything less than 1 is we are delayed and anything above 1 are we are ahead, and 1 means we are as per target.

Cost variation can be understood by looking at the completion of 7 tasks and its earned value and actual cost. Here we are not comparing with 10 tasks, instead for the 7 tasks we completed, what is the variation till now. We use (Earned Value – Actual Cost) to calculate Cost Variation, here it its (700 – 900), so -200$ is cost variance at this point in time. Negative here means we are over the budget. Cost Performance Index (CPI) is calculated using (Earned Value/Actual Value), in this case its (700/900), which is 0.77 and anything less than 1 is we are poor (over the budget).

At this point we understood on how we calculate the Schedule variation and cost variation, knowing this a project team might want to predict the final value at the time of completion (EAC – Estimate At Completion). To calculate this value, In case 1, we need to know the Estimate To Complete (ETC- cost from now on) which is, when there is huge deviation and the planned values are no longer useful, then we can go ahead to estimate the cost for pending tasks newly. In such case its, Actual Cost + ETC.

In our case if the final budget at completion is 5000$ and as of now we have already consumed 900$ and if the Estimate to Complete is giving us another 4500$ (new calculation for pending tasks). Then our Estimate At completion is 900+4500 = 5400 $ when compared to Budget at Completion (BAC)

In Second case where instead of redoing the estimation for subsequent tasks (instead of ETC), the project team may be comfortable to go ahead with the cost for the subsequent tasks, the reasons could be the deviation happened in the past is a rare case. Then we calculate Estimate at completion using, Actual Value + (Budgeted At Completion – Earned Value), in our case, 900+ (5000-700), which is 5200$

In third case, the team believes that the variation happened now, could be the kind of variation they will face in future also, then they can calculate EAC, using Actual Value + ((Budgeted At Completion – Earned Value)/CPI), in our case, (900 + ((5000- 700)/0.77)), which is 6484. Now we also know that why we calculated CPI earlier.

In Earned Value Analysis we have to careful in taking the % completion of tasks and bringing the Earned Value. Partially completed tasks should be calculated with clear guidelines and should not allow variations. MS project kind of tool allows us to calculate these values in better way.

Below given a Sample on calculation,

Time Period	Planned Value	Earned Value	Actual Cost	BAC	Schedule Variance	Cost Variance	SPI	CPI	ETC	EAC
12 Jun 13	100	100	100	700	0	0	1	1	600	700
14 Jul 13	200	200	220	700	0	-20	1	0.91	550	750
14 Aug 13	300	240	300	700	-60	-60	0.8	0.8	575	815
12 Sep 13	400	360	440	700	-40	-80	0.9	0.81	415	775
10 Oct 13	500			700						775
12 Nov 13	600			700						775
14 Dec 13	700			700						775

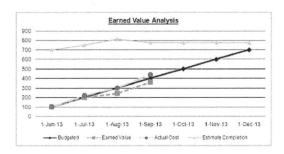

In this case, we can see that Estimate At Completion varies, as the other parameters Actual Cost and Earned Value vary.

19 REFERENCE SITES

a) www.cmmiinstitute.com

b) www.ISO.org

c) www.cosmicon.com

d) Seir.sei.cmu.edu

e) www.projectreference.com

f) www.asq.org

g) Sepo.spawar.navy.mil

h) www.rspa.com

i) Stattrek.com

j) Software.gsfc.nasa.gov/process.cfm

k) www.processimpact.com

l) www.sqaforums.com

m) www.crosstalkonline.org

n) Elsmar.com

www.ingramcontent.com/pod-product-compliance
Lightning Source LLC
LaVergne TN
LVHW022317060326
832902LV00020B/3514